OTHER VOLUMES IN THIS SERIES

THE
BEST
AMERICAN
POETRY
2004

◇ ◇ ◇

Lyn Hejinian, Editor

David Lehman, Series Editor

SCRIBNER POETRY

NEW YORK LONDON TORONTO SYDNEY

SCRIBNER POETRY
1230 Avenue of the Americas
New York, NY 10020

SCRIBNER POETRY and design are trademarks
of Macmillan Library Reference USA, Inc., used under license
by Simon & Schuster, the publisher of this work.

For information about special discounts for bulk purchases,
please contact Simon & Schuster Special Sales:
1-800-456-6798 or business@simonandschuster.com

Text Set in Bembo

Manufactured in the United States of America

1   3   5   7   9   10   8   6   4   2

Library of Congress Control Number: 88644281

ISBN 0-7432-5737-5
0-7432-5757-X (PBK)
ISSN 1040-5763

CONTENTS

THE
BEST
AMERICAN
POETRY
2004

◇ ◇ ◇

David Lehman was born in New York City in 1948. He is the author of five books of poems, including *The Daily Mirror* (2000) and *The Evening Sun* (2002), both from Scribner. Among his nonfiction books are *Signs of the Times: Deconstruction and the Fall of Paul de Man* (Simon & Schuster, 1991), *The Last Avant-Garde: The Making of the New York School of Poets* (Anchor, 1999), and *The Perfect Murder* (Michigan, 2000). He edited *Great American Prose Poems: From Poe to the Present*, which appeared from Scribner in 2003, and has served as general editor of the Poets on Poetry Series (University of Michigan Press) since 1994. He teaches writing and literature in the graduate writing programs of New School University in New York City and Bennington College in Vermont, and offers a course on "Great Poems" each fall at New York University. Now preparing a new edition of *The Oxford Book of American Poetry*, he initiated *The Best American Poetry* series in 1988 and received a Guggenheim Fellowship a year later. He lives in New York City and in Ithaca, New York.

FOREWORD

by David Lehman

◊ ◊ ◊

"Anthologies are, ideally, an essential species of criticism," wrote Randall Jarrell in *Poetry and the Age*. "Nothing expresses and exposes your taste so completely—nothing is your taste so nearly—as that vague final treasury of the *really* best poems that grows in your head all your life." Every reader is perennially compiling, enlarging, and revising such an anthology, which can never be "final" or definitive any more than a published anthology can be or should be exhaustive or complete. Anthologies are selective; they project an editor's taste, but they are also exercises in criticism. Their job is not only to reflect accurately what is out there but to pick and choose among the possibilities. Whether they set out to reinforce the prevailing taste or to modify it, they sometimes end up doing a bit of both. Anthologies can educate, can recruit new readers, can even create the conditions by which the new poetry may be savored and in time perhaps even understood, it being the usual case that enjoyment precedes understanding. All anthologies perform an evaluative function. Even where the claim is less absolute than in the title of *The Best American Poetry*, anthologies praise their contents. Donald Allen's *New American Poetry, 1945–1960*, the most influential anthology of the 1960s, which introduced a generation of readers to the Beats and Black Mountain, the New York School and the San Francisco Renaissance, may seem to have a neutral, descriptive title. But does anyone doubt that *new* here means *best*? Anthologies single out works worthy of perpetuation and as such they always constitute a prediction, an assertion, and a gamble.

Anthologies have played an even larger part in the education of modern poets than critics have noticed. Take the numerous poetry editions prepared by the long-lived Louis Untermeyer (1885–1977), who attained eminence despite dropping out of high school and working full-time in his father's jewelry business until he was thirty-eight. Untermeyer was a prolific poet and a skillful parodist, but his real talent went into his carefully annotated poetry compilations. Both John Ashbery and A. R. Ammons, guest editors of the 1988 and 1994 editions of *The Best American Poetry*, have spoken of the powerful effect that Untermeyer's anthologies had on them when they were young men. In grade school, Ashbery won a current events contest sponsored by *Time* magazine and received Untermeyer's *Modern American and British Poetry* as a prize. The volume taught him that verse need not rhyme, that the pleasures of Robert Frost and Elinor Wylie were easily had but that the more "baffling" pleasures of Auden and Dylan Thomas ultimately held more charm. It was an Untermeyer anthology, perhaps the same one, that the late A. R. Ammons discovered as a nineteen-year-old sailor on a U.S. Navy destroyer escort in 1945. Reading it felt like a rite of initiation: "I began to imitate those poems then, and I wrote from then on." A generation later, Untermeyer's anthologies were still in circulation. They had a great effect on me in my teens. To his *Concise Treasury of Great Poems* I owe my first acquaintance with Milton, Keats, Yeats, Frost, Eliot. I remember prizing the editor's running comments. He had an eye for the quirky biographical detail. From Untermeyer I learned, for example, that William Cullen Bryant's father, a country doctor in Cummington, Massachusetts, "attempted to reduce his son's abnormally large head by soaking it every morning in a spring of cold water" and that Bryant died in New York City at age eighty-four upon climbing a flight of stairs shortly after dedicating a statue to Mazzini in Central Park.

There are pitfalls in every anthologist's path. Some are more avoidable than others. The editor who includes his or her own work runs a grave risk. In a 1939 revision of an anthology originally compiled in 1922, Untermeyer put in five of his poems and wrote about himself in the third person: "In 1928 he achieved a lifelong desire by acquiring a farm, a trout-stream, and half a mountain of sugar-maples in the Adirondacks, where he lives when he is not traveling and lecturing. He loves to talk and listens with difficulty." About Untermeyer, E. E. Cummings wrote scornfully: "mr u will not be missed / who as an anthologist / sold the many on the few / not excluding mr u." (This was a sort of proleptic obituary: Untermeyer outlived Cummings by fifteen years.) Similar complaints were voiced against Oscar Williams, the inveterate anthologist whose books introduced the young Ashbery to the new (and in some cases now undeservedly forgotten) poetry of the 1940s. In a generally favorable review, Randall Jarrell pointed out that an Oscar Williams production contained nine of Oscar Williams's poems and five by Thomas

Hardy. "It takes a lot of courage to like your own poetry almost twice as well as Hardy's," Jarrell commented.

Some problems are inherent in the structure of any anthology. On what basis were these poems chosen, and not others? What claim can be made for these works? With what practical effect? The first question is the hardest to answer. The recognition of a great or even a very good poem precedes any articulation of reasons for the choice. A true lover of poetry will know it and savor it when the right thing comes along—though sometimes he or she may need the tug that anthologies and critical essays are supposed to provide. My own criteria as a reader begin with an insistent pleasure principle. "Pleasure is by no means an infallible critical guide, but it is the least fallible," W. H. Auden observed. There is fierce competition for the reader's attention, and where impatience may once have expressed itself only after pages, today you can lose your reader in your opening line. A poem must capture the reader before it can do anything else, and to do that it must give pleasure.

An anthology aspiring to represent the best work in the field requires faith and trust: the editor's faith that a serious general audience for poetry does exist; the reader's trust in the editor's judgment. From the start, the governing assumption of *The Best American Poetry* has been that poetry worthy of reading and reading again is being written in such quantity and of such variety that it would be possible for an annual volume showcasing it to live up to the series name. The challenge is not only to select that work but to present it so attractively that it will connect with readers who have the curiosity and the goodwill but lack the time and the access to the plethora of print and electronic magazines in which the new poetry is appearing.

There are anthologies that organize themselves by region, genre, gender, movement, theme. Some of these beg the question of quality. Enough for a poem to be written about zucchini to warrant its inclusion in a volume of vegetable poems. But with anthologies that do not thus delimit themselves—anthologies that would speak to an American audience generously conceived—we expect that criteria of excellence have been invoked if not necessarily explained and defended. Helen Vendler has written cogently against "historically representative anthologies" in which the aim is the comprehensive coverage of a given era. She noted that the first two volumes of a Library of America anthology devoted to twentieth-century American poetry added up to eighteen hundred pages: "So many feeble poets; so many non-moving poems; so many withered dictions; so many sterile experiments. And so much pretentiousness; so much well-meaning polemic; so much prose masquerading as poetry; so many dubious poetics." An unsympathetic person might say the same about many a poetry anthology, even one fourteen hundred pages shorter. But while I disagree with Vendler's assessment of the two volumes under review, I believe that a contemporary anthology invites ridicule in precisely these harsh terms if it professes to be value-free in the aesthetic sense, or if it subordinates poetry to sociology, ethics, or politics.

As people groan ritually at puns, even the cleverest ones, some guest editors of *The Best American Poetry* have balked at the word *Best* in the title. This may reflect a culture-wide distrust of hierarchy and anything smacking of elitism. Still, it is noteworthy that editors of similarly titled anthologies of essays and short stories seem to feel little of the compunction that the poets bring to the table. Open a book of the year's best stories or essays and you will not encounter an expression of misgivings about the enterprise. Whatever else it intimates, the poets' self-consciousness about the word "best" is an acknowledgment that there is nothing scientific about the process of selection, that reading and judging are subjective and partial, and that some terms are best used with invisible quote marks around them. Nevertheless, there is something to be said for taking a stand, making a claim. Year after year *The Best American Poetry* recognizes that competition often accompanies the creation of art, which is made by persons of complexity and ambition who compete not only with peers but with ancestors. To be chosen by an admired poet for inclusion in a book that has "best" in its title must feel like an honor to all but the most jaded, and it means something because the ratio of poems considered to poems chosen is so extraordinarily one-sided. Thousands of poems are read multiple times in order to arrive in the end at a choice seventy-five. "No poet or novelist wishes he were the only one who ever lived," Auden has written, "but most of them wish they were the only one alive, and quite a number fondly believe their wish has been granted." There's a lot of truth to that. But *The Best American Poetry* also shows that poets who may have little in common, who come from different regions or movements and espouse clashing ideas or traditions, can coexist to each other's benefit in a single book.

In a relativist universe, where to be nonjudgmental is sometimes held up as a great virtue, there may be something quixotic about an enterprise labeling itself "the best." The use of the word may be written off as an example of American hyperbole. But it seems to me that this anthology series is also an attempt to redefine "best" and render it credible by conceiving of each year's edition as initially a clean slate and ultimately an overhaul of the previous year's book. Each year a distinguished poet of national reputation does the selecting. The idea is not to fix a canon but to suggest possible orderings: to acknowledge that canons do not remain fixed for long, and to act on the notion by shifting perspective annually in surveying new poetry in print or electronic circulation. Each volume in the series records the encounters of one poet with the contents of many magazines in one twelve-month stretch. Place the volumes side by side on a shelf, and they also chronicle the taste and judgment of some of our leading poets.

Neal Bowers feels that there is something in the atmosphere of universities that jeopardizes our ability to separate good from bad, best from second-rate, and that the dependence of poets on academic institutions is therefore at the root of this problem as well as others. "To say that something is good or bad, beautiful or ugly, worthwhile or a waste of time is to 'privilege' one thing over another," he writes in the Summer 2003 issue of *Sewanee Review*. "Anyone who makes such distinctions had best keep his views to himself else he risk being tarred as a monocultural, nondiverse reactionary." Bowers, a recently retired university poet, was continuing a critique of the creative writing profession that he began a year earlier in the July 2002 issue of *Poetry*. "Students emerge from graduate writing programs with an understanding of poetry as something manufactured for the exclusive inspection of their peers," he laments. Bowers likes employing metaphors drawn from economics. There has been, he charges, an assault on standards with the result that "the undifferentiated supply [of poems] far outstrips demand." The university has a monopoly on poetry: "With a rate of success unmatched even by Wal-Mart, the university has driven almost all independent operations into ruin, controlling the production and distribution of poetry and regulating its worth."

The voicing of objections to the institution of the creative writing workshop is not exactly a groundbreaking event, but Bowers's essays are so obviously heartfelt that they seem worthy of consideration. Though there may be elements of caricature in his description of how writing programs work, he would do us a service nonetheless if his essays provoked students and teachers in MFA programs to mount a defense of what they do. When Bowers argues that writing programs mark "the transformation of poetry from a passion to a professional undertaking," he makes me want to challenge the dichotomy. Why can't poetry be both a passion and a serious professional undertaking? Aren't our best teachers those who inspire and sustain the young poet's passion for the art—and do so in a professional manner? Bowers attacks the notion that the only career path available to an MFA student is as a teacher in an MFA program. "Because poetry matters in and of itself and not as an aspect of employment, [people] can make time to write, whatever job they do to earn an income," he says. I agree. *Go forth into the world* is good advice. But Bowers's plea for "poetry professors" to rise up as one and renounce the "concept and common practices of the poetry workshop" is as absurd as it is unlikely to happen. To ditch the workshop is to ditch the writing programs' raison d'être as well as their most popular and effective structural innovation. Bowers reasons that instructors can reinvent themselves as old-fashioned literature professors. "Because their English-department colleagues have abandoned literature in favor of literary theory, poet-professors could seize the opportunity to restore the reading and discussion of literature." But writing programs do require their students to study the literature of the past; they can perhaps do it better, or more rigorously, but they do it, they keep literature alive as a subject of study and as an indispensable concomitant of the creative imagination. A bad workshop is going to be as painful and wasteful as any failed pedagogical endeavor. A good workshop can change your life.

Poets have recently given us new versions of Dante, *Beowulf*, *Sir Gawain and the Green Knight*, Aeschylus' *Oresteia*, Sophocles' *Philoctetes*. And poets, whether they come from the ranks of writing programs or not, will contrive new ways to perpetuate the many traditions, movements, schools, and personalities that are conjoined in modern poetry. It is important that poetry have a base in the university. It is even better to find poetry in shops, cafés, bars, and clubs; spilling into the street; entering people's lives. This anthology series is predicated on the profoundly democratic notion that there are readers out there, in some cases far from museums and libraries, who are desperate for poetry to be in their lives.

Lyn Hejinian and I met at a poetry conference in Copenhagen in August 2001. Our Danish hosts had hoped that she and I would come to blows on a panel at which it was thought that she would represent the Language School and I the New York School in a debate. Instead we began a dialogue that lasted months, took different forms on different continents, and gave us both, I think, much pleasure. I knew in what great esteem she is held by the many young writers who consider her autobiographical sequence, *My Life*, to be a modern masterpiece. "I saw a juxtaposition /

It happened to be between an acrobat and a sense of obligation / Pure poetry," she wrote in "Nights," a group of "night thoughts intended as an homage to Scheherazade," which Robert Hass picked for the 2001 edition of this anthology. I felt that this respected and admired writer with her eye for poetry, pure and otherwise, would make an excellent choice to serve as guest editor of this year's *Best American Poetry*, and I am glad I enlisted her. The Berkeley-based Hejinian threw herself into the task, reading as generously as she could while remaining true to her esthetic convictions and her commitment to poetry of a high experimental bent. One reason the volume is exciting is its strong accent on youth. But we also rejoice in the fact that a book containing a poem written by a high school senior (Marc Jaffee, now an undergraduate at Vassar) also contains a poem by Carl Rakosi, the Objectivist poet who celebrated his hundredth birthday in 2003. Above all, there is satisfaction in knowing that the contents of this book represent a coherent vision of what one important poet considers to be American poetry at its most vital, daring, and aggressively new.

In 2003 Louise Glück became the nation's twelfth poet laureate, succeeding Billy Collins in the post. Glück, who edited the 1993 volume in this series, has made few pronouncements in her new official capacity. She has given us a new poem instead: the beautiful *October*, published as a chapbook by Sarabande. It is a quiet and intimate poem and it has nothing political in it, yet it seems to have a public dimension, speaking to all who can identify themselves with that time of year when the light begins to fail and yellow leaves or none or few still cling to branches. At the end of the poem we reach the ultimate condition of lyric poetry: the lonely self contemplating the naked universe.

> From within the earth's
> bitter disgrace, coldness and barrenness
>
> my friend the moon rises:
> she is beautiful tonight, but when is she not beautiful?

The publication of such a poem—or of seventy-five of them, gleaned from a year's intense reading—creates the place where the private consciousness of the creative mind intersects with its most generous impulses toward community.

Lyn Hejinian was born in the San Francisco Bay Area in 1941. A poet, essayist, and translator, she is the author or coauthor of more than two dozen books of poetry, including *The Fatalist* (Omnidawn, 2003), *The Beginner* (Spectacular Books, 2002), *A Border Comedy* (Granary Books, 2001), *Happily* (Post-Apollo Press, 2000), *The Cold of Poetry* (Sun and Moon Press, 1994), *The Cell* (Sun and Moon Press, 1992), and *My Life* (Sun and Moon Press, 1987). *The Language of Inquiry*, a collection of her critical essays, was published by the University of California Press in 2001. She has collaborated on numerous projects with other poets such as Leslie Scalapino, Kit Robinson, Jack Collom, Barrett Watten, Ray Di Palma, and Carla Harryman. From 1976 to 1984, Hejinian was editor of Tuumba Press, and for seventeen years beginning in 1981 she was the coeditor of *Poetics Journal*. She is also the codirector of the literary press Atelos, which commissions and publishes cross-genre work by poets. For her translations from the Russian poet Arkadii Dragomoschenko, she received a grant from the National Endowment for the Arts. In 2000 she was awarded the sixty-sixth Fellowship from the Academy of American Poets for distinguished poetic achievement at mid-career. She lives in Berkeley and teaches at the University of California.

INTRODUCTION

by Lyn Hejinian

◊ ◊ ◊

This volume, *The Best American Poetry 2004*, is the seventeenth in a series, and it is precisely in its being an ongoing *series* that the *Best American Poetry* undertaking has, to my mind, its particular interest and value. Implicit in its being a series is an awareness that the story of American poetry is never, in any single period of its activity, complete, and no set of examples from a single year of it can possibly reveal all that is under way in its unfolding. Dynamic, ever-changing, poetry (and American poetry in particular) is a site of perpetual transitions and unpredictable metamorphoses, but there is no end point in poetry. Indeed, American poetry has always been so full of energy and so inventive that it is impossible to define poetry once and for all or to delimit its space. What is, or isn't, a poem? What makes something poetic? These questions remain open. And the fact that there are no final answers is one source of the vitality of the art form.

Certainly no single poem in this volume is definitive, nor is any single volume in *The Best American Poetry* series—not of "bestness," nor of what's "American," nor of "poetry"; and, if this particular volume is in any way typical, none of the volumes are even definitive of their guest editor's aesthetics or poetics nor even of his or her "tastes," though I must say that I myself have learned something about mine (and about the necessity of querying and opposing them) in the course of reading through and selecting from many of the more than many poetry-publishing magazines and journals, online and on paper, that came out during the past year.

Reading through that wondrous (and, in this era of censure and censorship, often defiant) array of diverse, historically interrelated, and still autonomous literary magazines published in 2003, I gained access to powerful and engaged counters to the doleful state of the year, in the work not only of the poets published in those magazines but also in that of their dedicated, principled, and often visionary editors.*

Some American poetry magazines have institutional support, which means that some entity (often the English department or creative writing program of a college or university) provides the editor with some funds and/or office space and/or personnel (for example, a student assistant). More often, the magazines are the creation of an individual editor, who is almost invariably him- or herself a poet. Poetry is popularly believed to be a solitary undertaking, and the writing of it generally is. But the life of poetry is highly social; every poem acquires its meaning (and its meaningfulness) within the communities of those who care enough to consider it and converse about it. The editing of poetry magazines (like the curating of poetry readings) is a vastly important element in the creation and sustenance of those meaning-making communities.

It is also a labor of love. To edit a poetry magazine will get one neither fame nor money. What one gets are unexpectedly high printers' bills, heaps of unsolicited manuscripts, and the task of getting the magazine out to readers. One also gets the pleasure of knowing that one is helping to invent one's times.

What is best in American poetry is, finally, all of it, in all its modes and moods and themes and divagations. It is written and published against the logics dominating the times, and it flourishes—in no small part thanks to the editors of poetry magazines. To all those editors I wish to pay my personal tribute and to them I dedicate my share in the compiling of this volume.†

The Best American Poetry series offers a display of sorts rather than a delineation, but of course that display is the product of multiple evaluations. The evaluations entailed, however, are variously motivated and variously contextualized, and what can be seen unfolding in the series (and in this volume, I hope, as a small part of it) is a history, but one that

---

*Lest poetry published late in any given year get overlooked, the "Best" editor is given some retrospective leeway, and thus, to be absolutely accurate, for this volume I also read through some magazines published in late 2002.

†For anyone interested, various lists of current literary magazines are available. Among the best are the *International Directory of Little Magazines and Small Presses* (see dustbooks.com for information), the list provided online by Poets & Writers, Inc. (at pw.org), and, for people interested in experimental and innovative writing in particular, the poet Spencer Selby's online list (at selbyslist.com) is invaluable.

is heuristic in character, self-reflexive, arbitrarily completed annually (at seventy-five poems), and always ongoing. It is a phenomenological as well as a literary history—a history of encounters, between the series' guest editors, magazine editors, poets, poetry, and the year in question—in my case, the sorry year of 2003. It is especially that "sorriness" that seems to have exerted its demands on the choices that are revealed here.

This is "American poetry" and the year I speak of therefore is the "American" 2003. I don't intend here to expand on what that means to me, and I don't require readers to have felt the panics of frustration and fear that I have in the face of the various nefarious policies that the American government of 2003 perpetrated. But I must say that I cannot imagine a person, not to mention an artist and especially not a poet, who in the year 2003 could in her or his work have simply disregarded what's been going on—or, to use the apter phrase of the 1960s, to have disregarded what's been "going down."

There are, however, many ways of regarding the rampantly destructive character of so many of the year's events. And though I often found myself finding "bestness" in aggressive and/or overtly defiant works, I also found it in works offering fantasies (though not escapist ones) of alternatives, even alternatives of themselves. I found "bestness" in dislogical poems and in dialogical ones, and I found it in poems in which quixotic pathos is revolutionized into play. I found it in works long enough to sustain negativity and form a relationship with the world in negativity's terms, and I found it in the strange cosmological positives produced at unexpected points of encounter.

Initially I had qualms about taking on the editorship. My problem was simple and, going by what the editors of some of the previous volumes in this series have said in their own introductions, it seems to have vexed many of us. I don't believe in "bestness." I don't believe that one can dehistoricize and decontextualize cultural production and come up with anything that isn't stripped of a large measure of its liveliness. Isolation in the realm of bestness does, of course, tend to focus attention on a poem's beauty. But it has been said, and in my view truthfully, that "From beauty no road leads to reality. . . . The power of beauty affects the naked human being, as though he had never lived,"* and both a forced separation from reality and deprivation of living I would find insupportable, in art as much as in life. Surely we don't want to establish

*Hannah Arendt, *Rahel Varnhagen*, 88–89.

aesthetic conditions that deny the world and leave us feeling that we (or, indeed, the poem) have never lived.

Art is all about living, and its meanings do not emerge or reside (and certainly they cannot thrive) in the kind of isolation that "bestness" normally confers. Poetry, furthermore, is not a static art form—its sources of energy (its virtues) are not frozen in perfection but flow through time as consciousness and question. Just as meaning in language is created by the linking together of strings of words into phrases and sentences, so the meaning in poetry is created by the linking together of poems to form the large, ancient, and ever new human undertaking of thinking together about the things that matter to us.

As the poet Jack Spicer once said, in a frequently quoted letter to Robin Blaser, "The trick naturally is what [Robert] Duncan learned years ago and tried to teach us—not to search for the perfect poem but to let your way of writing of the moment [or, I would add, of reading] go along its own paths, explore and retreat but never be fully realized (confined) within the boundaries of one poem. . . . There is really no single poem." "Poems should echo and reecho against each other," he continued. "They should create resonances. They cannot live alone any more than we can."

It is precisely that kind of "bestness"—the common good of being lively—that I hope this volume in *The Best American Poetry* series celebrates.

The history of poetry anthologies is long and fascinating; indeed, anthologies themselves tend each to be long (*The Best American Poetry* volumes are an exception to this rule) and they of course hope (this one not excepted) to be fascinating. There are various identifiable types of anthologies. Some are intended to stand as monuments to an era or to a movement; these are retrospective and their aim is to be definitive. Some are intended to announce that something is happening; these are forward-looking and their aim is to inform (or perhaps to reform) the world, to fuel excitement, and to defy the dubious. Some (and some of the best) are compendia or "mere" miscellanies; *The Greek Anthology* is a superb example of the former, *Tottel's Miscellany* of the latter, but one might also include such books as Francis T. Palgrave's 1861 anthology, *The Golden Treasury*, and, much more recently, Jorie Graham's *Earth Took of Earth*, in this category.

Though the contents of this volume are strictly limited to poems published in America within a given twelve-month period, it too is intended as a miscellany of sorts. And yet, even in its miscellaneousness, it tells a story; it presents a picaresque adventure (the volume begins with the escape of a small figure onto its opening page) across innumerable sites and through diverse situations. This is a good story. It has no moral (morals tend to discourage thinking and the poetry here strongly favors thinking), but it is rich in experiences and full of reality, full of world.

Reality, of course, always exceeds even the best poems; there is always more world than a writer can create, or represent, or speak of, or, even, reject. But, paradoxically, it is also true that poems sometimes exceed the world; there are places in them that create nothing, that represent nothing, that speak of nothing, that reject nothing. This "nothing" is a thing we can't know; all our knowing is of something. Yet poetry is fascinated by the unknown, which it often finds full of meaning.

Encounters with meaning (and with it, the sense of meaningfulness) bring with them the emotion of making sense, i.e., of discovering sense or, sometimes and with a stronger emotion, of having created sense. For me, the poems in this volume are informed by that kind of strong emotion. They make sense in a year that one can scarcely make sense of.

There remains something to be said about how to read this book, and I will begin by saying that I hope it will be read *as* a book. The seventy-five poems follow each other alphabetically, according to the last name of the seventy-five authors. Thus I, as the book's editor, cannot take any credit for the extraordinary resonances that exist between adjacent poems as one moves through the sequence—but those resonances exist. And I would suggest that they, like the poems themselves, invite us to read this work not from the point of view of spectators but from that of artists.

To engage with art as the artist has done is to take an inventive and activist role rather than a passive and consumerist one. What interests the artist is the working—the interested living, not the disinterested spectatorship.

Even as the discourse in and of political life is being shrunk into something harrowingly "patriotic," the poems here should be read, separately and together, as expansive interactions. It is often thought that desire drives us to yearn to possess the objects of our desire. But how unlike poetry that is! We capture nothing in words. The desire that propels poetry propels us away from our "possessions" and forth into the world, replete with realities, from the rocks underfoot to our dreams.

Side by side

simultaneously

the world

in its
          types
fragments

     (pulling)

          the surface, tension
          lower parts

     power the wind, echo,
     sound like the beach

          variety

     we are apt to forget

          planes

     at the angles

The woman talks to her dog
and I bark

          irons of sand
                    one
     atom to an experiment

          Larry Eigner, 1927–1996,
          from *Things Stirring Together or Far Away*

Chicken

◇　◇　◇

Why did she cross the road?
She should have stayed in her little cage,
shat upon by her sisters above her,
shitting on her sisters below her.

God knows how she got out.
God sees everything. God has his eye
on the chicken, making her break
like the convict headed for the river,

sloshing his way through the water
to throw off the dogs, raising
his arms to starlight to praise
whatever isn't locked in a cell.

He'll make it to a farmhouse
where kind people will feed him.
They'll bring green beans and bread,
home-brewed hops. They'll bring

the chicken the farmer found
by the side of the road, dazed
from being clipped by a pickup,
whose delicate brain stem

he snapped with a twist,
whose asshole his wife stuffed
with rosemary and a lemon wedge.
Everything has its fate,

but only God knows what that is.
The spirit of the chicken will enter the convict.
Sometimes, in his boxy apartment,
listening to his neighbors above him,

annoying his neighbors below him,
he'll feel a terrible hunger
and an overwhelming urge
to jab his head at the television over and over.

from *Five Points*

from *Solea of the Simooms*

◇　◇　◇

surprise . . . *will burst forth like a fluorite ruby in ultraviolet light*
—Roberto Matta

Not some writhing in a tortuous canine province
nor some hallucinated witness starving in a broken endocrine manger
but Solea
the splendiferous dolorosos of Solea
with her blind electrical surges
with her transmundane penetration
like a rain of green sorrows
with their clairvoyant ethers
become a cyclone of minerals
ghostly
eclectic
like a moon expelling waves from her dharma

or movement from the carving of volcanoes

her electric punctuation
condensed
as neutrino & anti-neutrino
with the earth as her dazzled village
with its brush fire error
with its radiant electrokinetic mass
like a cell as inverted doctrine
or body as hydraulic solar current

movement
has become her speaking in formal hoodoo or Formosan
much like a Spanish lynx
or the howl of an Asiatic lion
circular
as in an acid
lurking in strange bacteria

her mesmerism
her antiphonal hailstorm prism
like a form of dust in pure imaginary linkage
much like the soil in bloodless dromedary trance
or cups of fire
or kinetic trays of snow

like an ice bound tornado
or a frozen ballet of minimums
or blazeless corruptible sullage
she sings within the distance of subverted salamander flowers

one could speak of her multiple incendiary foliage
blazing
as a kind of poisonous tantra
or a voice from heated voltage sierras

she invokes in me
forms which preceded human electrical formation
such as the Ammonites
the Brachiopods
the Medusina
expressing movement
beyond the terminal insinuendos of being
beyond the ragged palpitations of a cautious dissembling liberty
in which the isometric instinct devolves
& the surge of the pre-edenic persists
across splintered unifications
condensed as rotational spectra
arising in optical sodium
in ionized hydrogen grammes

so if I form a perpendicular mass as regards her
or if I form a condensation
or a sudden Hydroxyl in her favour
I will know
that the gulfs burn
the biopsies detach
the nebulas roam

then the ionic fall of the solar expanse
will take on a powerful enigma as drone

& never will be debased
by a motionless treason
by squalls which collapse through resistance

because carbon elliptically rotates
across the grass of a burning sonar basin
she sings as if swimming
in a dark apportional heat
in a dazzled background lime
in the deserts or swamps of the veins
in a microscopic medical leaf
then equating these blazes with wise subjective errata

her fleeting sonar crystals
culled from intermolecular force
like verbal nitrogen writing
a draft
oblique
stunning
of coded immaterial flaw
never once being subjected
to the perplexing hail
in a depthless fractional sentence
her voice being essence
as in lakeless mysteriums of ubiquity
as in biologic drift
in its drones
in its lines of perceptive randomity

& so I can speak of her fraternization of coils
of her of graph as a floating background species
much like fluid from pillaged mongoose seeds

so should I come to myself with a dossier of blankness
should I address an assemblage of beings in viharas
I could never blind myself to Solea
to her distance
to her subcontinents inside snowfall

no
& I am not speaking for the quest for dialectical frondage
but movement which sweeps across a narrowed wall of flux
across foundational pathology
yet spinning above a garish vulture's milk

one thinks of fevers
of drawls
of quiescence
of burnings

then the nerves
the chants
the quaking motor flows

my hearing
focused upon songs about thirstless cranial doves
about the listless erasures of panic
like a tragic mystical salt
within an incandescent bravery

& such bravery
is the colour of rhizomes & multiples
much like a splintered nebula as food

her phonation flies
throughout the "high refractive index" of diamonds
with their separated flairs
with their special carbon ideals
become the motion in sound which floats

from blind incarnadine zephyrs
wafting above molten flowing in "Minas Gerais"

her voice producing seeming confines of sterling
being propertied in balance
amidst a bleak doctrinal ruse
she then becomes like a dancer
with black equestrian vivacity

from *No: a journal of the arts*

from *Dang Me*

◊ ◊ ◊

3.

A rumble with complacency, a bestiality beyond barking squash proclivity cherry — stupendous infraction. A disassembled kissing shame as pick-me-up — martial doggone awful pesto pindrop powwow debutarts tighten up your resumé sphincter living for a better suicide.

Peter expressive poptop tutors sizing lambing mutants' code of silence; hit me for monkey smack freak. Maudlin in lab rat out your relatives, superego-abrogated pre-amp fit prize prissy quickset scold. When you do inch your regret as a sissy massage your willpower conceited whip always offended by the (mostly guys') encoding of arcane sports lore (mostly baseball) in their poems. Vivisectional sofas sentimental with regard to length of neck. Are you: related to anyone who was subject to a famous autopsy? The insouciant schizo wants a biscuit.

No, dirt aliens: don't waste good mascara, fiber gives you confidence. Spin doctors vs. gravity, do you spandex wooden leg plus spaz hemp tempi seize the fey crawlspatiality creatures peel off. Barbie protons slobber the manual seedling wrapped in human skin. Happy puppy preconscious vouchers don't brownnose your pal's girlfriend, a swagger unanointed affect in its gob phase. Automated preparation H — a nongoosing, a midriff melody — stir the rack up . . . mere child has her permit.

Orphan floodlit self-injury as a nurse stalking technique. Doll, pucker up. Behaving goosestep pedo-foo-foo bambi freezer, corsage murk inept debby queer hurt eyebrows could tell idle hands make the best poison.

The gotcha with spongy, heart-shaped puddling effect — robots grading too easy on the verification procedures. You, as in warning erotic silo squeeze tutorial, the pliable rubbable huggable bra rat. Swallowing makes you thirsty to like bugspray = siblings in burnbag. Ego gets rich yeah sudden substud dodderism, a self-reeducation camp award ceremony expels me. Your diamonds stay alert & even the selfless get jealous. Cheetah change, extrapodiatrical; bon vivant give & take *de ville* in the flesh. When do the slutty prefer to think of your apartment as a graveyard so live an endless summer . . . not that anything much matters.

4.

Ringing anthemic lies — unpack sizzle thumping hammer sparks as fun stuff & slip it off. Collective butcher shop projections festoon on your desk, truly uneventful habitat disinclined to be contritionally restored. Motive bodega bjork hole portishead squirt at the squint — don't make me big sarcastic forbearance skirting the turkeybeat. Husband admits to rental nimbus slutted on history. Mumble the surviving, translate the howdy — promotion got me perpetual perjury machine, narcotic-oblivious piglets in open court. Frighten the blouse pulp overbite, party-favored pocket disasterdom pseudo-enacters enjoy.

All the squeeze play in the world sideshow is busy soft whoops your wampum versa vice, both barrels. Videotic fuss only surveil guys veer toward peewee talent as splay flab out of stir: which part of speech heckled you? Fluoridating the acoustics, a smash cast mega telekineme — magma performative dinosaur bits just as effortless.

Rabid wishers pick & choose plural munch to auto-patrol their assurances. Stun such spellbünd. Talk gives up a greasier monitoring: mega-playgrounds & meta-playgrounds, preposterous polyappropriaters — didn't we — just carefree — couldn't we — training. Learn alienation; anger gets sorry — crankhead uplift little problem. Old Vernacular Home, a heavily insured exhalation butters your coffee. CRUCIAL: Let more shit roll off our backs.

We don't have ancestors, we have creditors. YaknowwhatI'msayin'. What I want is a tiny wireless clip-on digital microphone with a remote firewire connection to Voice Recognition software (with near-perfect success in producing text — better than the current OCR software on scanners) onto my desktop — as if any extended syntactical effort generated an overstrong whiff of surrealism. The fuzzies are gone; lick me some nash. Vernacular nosedive stuff is inducted dandy then verisimilitude, your examples wearing hippie fringe. Venereal industriousness to target inculcation privilege, ironic serial killing science for backpackers' manichean mook pompous scare gonna fin-de-siècle it.

Don't be first person phobic savaged by the unattainable. Keep your machines fit to obsolesce ideologue doggedness — predicantored ballroom chamois chicanery spelunking scratchier sops nanodiscourse to become stealth fantasy. The blood wants to be on a uniform a condom can misapprehend.

5.

Let's erase your purpose: policy geek-ozoa, lock 'n' rote a limbo *chi minh* chingaling — *menial leisure,* thumpy leech. A taste's club of social democracy pretenders, one little posse cognitively refried monads of fire, handsomer in handcuffs, to give birth to = to push drugs on. Pixie prexie squeezing the getters — could we have a half boldface — tortoisey vanguard vacillate caricature pork rezips flack-jacketed daydreams' curare in redeemer's neck self-stabilizing class relations.

Nice force! — so much more to life than political incorrectness whiffing off your armistice. No more boning it alone cohabit purple rain crackfest presence takes a crack at race — do I get the replaceable skill sets? Aristotelos shiny waste *polizei* fast führered pork shock gobble gobble fun slots rearranged, giblets of empire chilling integer edges — you need prehab in qualcom flips. Failing collective efficacy, we tend to our individual careers; failing in our careers, we tend to our individual leisure pasttimes — powdery, in kit form. Victory greed to endrool, lizardskinny dot com minus visa moors catty demon lamb dumbo praxis broke up productively. Satanic civil rights — kiss your placebo goodbye! Families that get high together got promoted from Veterans Day to Memorial Day, just by dying: ever more restless sublime forever works off its particle. One long procession of cherrytops designing a vacancy, war-mongerer's phones are down. I highlight the decade, clicked delete & it just goes away. This politics of memory, pretty easy — all those historically mediated diapers take the Tory out of "improvisatory."

Slant fit deep-pocketed triage, reversible killjoy kiss-off or kick-back dissonant and/or untuned pseudo-outreach backdrop to mammon tourniquet debut. MONEY WILD — WORLD PERKS, they don't expire. Riot on credit, the smear rehabitates past Presidents all communing around the ritual pipe the Formerly Free World will agitate for cash. We can't oversize blowbacks: think of the Third World as a Fundraiser. Municipality interrumptus, bubbly supply-siders yelling into a lonely beaker you recover from . . . serial murder & move to the suburbs. No lifestyle means no condom, puke for our touch. Restove the prex goo hunch wolf ceiling why oath boomboom mounties rejazz yourself.

How much do you really want to denigrate the scope & depth of knowledge (not just data — i.e., unmanaged information) held by fans of pop stuff you don't care for (bands, stars, sports, etc.). Blood well-behaved bozo corporation — any skinny tie'll do. Blackmail, request backup. All you need is wingtips like you mean business — time as a knee offering, a transference anti-colloidal health, that circus trick. Metacorporate morphine scruples made from the sugar cubes of Scrooge McDuck diving into the swimming pool full of paper money. Treat me as well as your pets.

from *SHINY*

Almost

◊   ◊   ◊

1

Almost all the words we've said to one another are gone
and if they were retrieved, verbatim, we might not acknowledge them.
But the *tenor* of our talk
has been constant across decades!
(Tenor is what we meant by "soul.")

For instance,
the way we joke
by using non-sequiturs, elliptical remarks
which deliberately suppress context
in advance
of time's rub-out.

2

"When size really counts,"
the billboard says

showing the product
tiny,

in one corner,

so we need to search for it.
Come find me.

I stand
behind these words.

from *Mississippi Review*

CRAIG ARNOLD

Your friend's arriving on the bus

◊　◊　◊

at six a.m.　　and you will go to meet her
because you are your own puppet
can stop bullets　　and you would never
get lost　　the street map of the world
is wired into your brain　　and anyway
it is all a big adventure　　and the wrong
bus station　　but you don't know that yet

Here is the statue of Queen What's-her-name
green with a copper-polished nose
Here is the market but no vegetables
The stalls are boarded up and look
uncomfortable　　Here is the cathedral
Here is the square　　smack in the middle
here is the couple fucking　　half-undressed
skin on the flagstone　　Isn't it cold
Couldn't they find even a patch of grass

Here is the bus station　　Where are the buses
Why are the windows all so starry-eyed
A bus would be too sad to come here

Here is a man falling in step beside you
dark　　his hair is full of eagles
Spare change he says　　You give him some
No not enough　　he says　　but you don't have

anything more to give him   *No I want*
your wallet   *Yes your wallet*   *I've got a*
something   What the something is
you don't appreciate   remember this
is all in Spanish   probably something sharp
Why don't you run   *Don't run*   he calls
across three lanes of traffic and the strip
of grass between them and the three
lanes of traffic going the other way
Lucky for you there aren't too many cars

Two garbagemen are working down the street
in orange uniforms   They look
conspicuous   better to walk beside them
looking   you hope   conspicuous   at least
by association   They don't seem to mind

Perhaps you are too tall for walking
Here you hail a cab and tell the driver
The bus station please   and not that one
the other bus station   do you know where
and he says *No   why don't we check*
the phone book   You've been here six months
and never seen a phone book   but no doubt
he has a better idea of where to find one
being a cab driver   and one would hope
knowledgeable about such things
Besides you need to find an ATM
You don't have any money left to pay him

Here is a bar   phone book cash and coffee
all together   What a stroke of luck
All set to rumble   but now the driver
gets in an argument about the Basques
bombing another car   you so hate
to interrupt   and it is only after
three cups of coffee that all parties
are satisfied
                You'd like to meet the Basques
They look like they are into heavy metal

and have ideas about destruction
Maybe your mugger was a Basque
and that was why you didn't understand
the something
                    Here is the station and her bus
has just pulled up to the platform
hours late   What timing   if you had gone
straight to the right place you would have only
waited for hours   and not been
so wonderfully abstracted by the Basques
the fare   the phone book   and the orange men
and the running away in sheer adrenal terror
from the mugger with that something you will spend
hours over the dictionary
hoping to decode
                    and yes those two
not minding where they made a kind of love

Of course you could have eaten breakfast
smoked a pack of the nasty cigarettes
and made new words to songs
The pain in Spain falls mainly on the sane
or some such variation   and no doubt
time would have run on swimmingly

Isn't it sweet when everything works out

from *Open City*

JOHN ASHBERY

Wolf Ridge

◇   ◇   ◇

Attention, shoppers. From within the inverted
commas of a strambotto, seditious whispering
watermarks this time of day. Time to get out
and, as they say, about. Becalmed on a sea
of inner stress, sheltered from the cold northern breezes,
idly we groove: Must have
been the time before this, when we all moved
in schools, a finny tribe, and this way
and that the caucus raised its din:
punctuation and quips, an "environment"
like a lovely shed. My own plastic sturgeon
warned me away from knowing. Now see the damage.
You can't. It's invisible. Anyway, you spent his love,
swallowed everything with his knives,
a necessary unpleasantness viewed from the rumble seat
of what was roaring ahead.

I want to change all that.
We came here with a mandate of sorts, anyway
a clear conscience. Attrition and court costs
brought you last year's ten best. Now it's firm
and not a bit transparent. Everybody got lost
playing hide and seek, except you,
who were alone. Not a bad way to end the evening,
whistling. They wanted a bad dinner,
and at this time a bad dinner was late.
Meatloaf, you remembered, is the third vegetable.

from *Conjunctions*

MARY JO BANG

The Eye
Like a Strange Balloon
Mounts Toward Infinity

◊   ◊   ◊

We were going toward nothing
all along. Honing the acoustics,
heralding the instant
shifts, horizontal to vertical, particle

to plexus, morning to late,
lunch to later yet, instant to over. Done
to overdone. And all against
a petstore cacophony, the roof withstanding

its heavy snow load. So, winter. And still,
ambition to otherwise and a forest of wishes.
Meager the music floating over. The car
in the driveway. In the P-lot, or curbside.

A building overlooking an estuary,
inspired by a lighthouse.
Always asking, Has this this been built?
Or is it all process?

Molecular coherence, a dramatic canopy,
cafeteria din, audacious design. Or humble.
Saying, We ask only to be compared to the ant-
erior cruciate ligament. So simple. So elegant.

Animated detail, data from digital.
But of course there is also longstanding evil.
The spider speaking
to the fly, Come in, come in.

Overcoming timidity. Overlooking
consequence. Finally ending
with the future. Take comfort.
You were going nowhere. You were not alone.

You were one
of a body curled on a beach. Near sleep
on a balcony. The negative night
in a small town or part of an urban abstraction.

Looking up
at the billboard hummingbird,
its enormous beak. There's a song that goes . . .
And then the curtain drops.

> Odilon Redon, *The Eye Like a*
> *Strange Balloon Mounts Toward Infinity*,
> charcoal on paper, 1882

from *Ploughshares*

20 Questions

◊   ◊   ◊

What can be said of the unspeakable that has not already been unsaid

What kind of pill does it take

Is outliving enemies a hollow victory

Can moonlight prevent the leaves from stirring

How many presidents say "nucular" instead of "nuclear"

Is the brain constructed from activity

How is life on the natch

Is solid eye contact critical to being a hit

Who would fardels bear

What is the statute of limitations

Do you know you've arrived when carts are free

Do we get all the help we need from arithmetic

Who is as tickled as a dog with two dicks

Does something for everyone mean nothing for anyone

Would you be kind enough

How many lightbulbs does it take to change the world

Are you in this for the overalls

Do fine feathers make fine birds

Remember when a million was a billion

Can what they call civilization be right if people mayn't die in the room
where they were born

from *SHINY* and *The Forward*

Sign Under Test

◇　◇　◇

On an evening in June, alone with anxious mediations, reading by mobbed light, I come again, taste to taste, with my own self-inoculations.

Paying double but taking only half.

As swill becomes saunter.

The sky lies so the dirt can give the boot.

Then again, there are certain things I never understood, yet lately I find myself mesmerized by these blank spots. They have become the sign posts of my consciousness.

The old becomes new again when it arrives after whatever is recent and seems fresh. On the other hand, nothing is so old as that which comes after but seems as if it must have been from before.

It's so quiet you can hear the lint festering in the fog.

I'll give you a hand but only one.

Fighting fire with sugar to make pie while the hay dries in the oyster-man's holiday.

Winter tears, summer shadows.

Poetry is patterned thought in search of unpatterned mind.

Love is the messenger not the message.

Till you get to the backside of where you began. Neither round robin nor oblong sparrow.

My faculties are impolitic.

But at least: For two dimes and a nickel you still get something like a quarter.

Sometimes a gust is just a gust.

The ghosts just left.

That still, small voice may not be the root of all evil but it's no innocent bystander either.

There's tackle in the tackle box.

How can you separate the breach from the brook, the branch from the book?

The haze doesn't obscure the view it makes it palpable.

It's not the absence in the presence but the presence in the absence.

When you go away there's no back to come back to. All the addresses have changed and the locks have new combinations.

A husband returns home to find a burning cigar in his ashtray. He soon discovers a man in the broom closet. "What are you doing there?" — "Everybody's got to be somewhere." [Henny Youngman]

Rabbi Eliza asks, "When is a Jew no longer a Jew?" — "When the book is closed."

The pit of the cherry is like the soul of a self-righteous man: when you find it, you want to spit it out.

The slips have become skirts.

The dove cannot find rest for the soul of its foot. Neither can I find peace in the inner worlds beside the nearby.

Inoperative nomenclature.

A series of hints without a question, a slew of clues without a crime.

Why did the turtle cross the road? — To find the chicken.

What you don't know's a far cry from what you do.

Desperately searching for a book that I don't even want to read.

"The world is everything that is the case." But the case is locked in the trunk of a stolen car.

Everything that happens is lost. Even what is recalled is lost in the recalling. Nonetheless, things go on happening.

Memory is to life like a band-aid to a wound.

A girl I once met told me her name rhymed with orange.

Did I just imagine that?

Complexity is a ten-letter word, like difficulty. There's moxie in complexity and tilt in difficulty but what difference does this make?

I'll give you ten minutes and if you don't come out I'll give you ten more minutes.

My cares turned to wares.

Simply stated, there's nothing to state.

It's not what you say that counts nor what you don't say but the relation.

He understated the price of the property to be sure he got less than it was worth. This was the only way he knew for the exchange to have value.

Give me a place to sit and I will look for a place to put up my feet.

TILT

Everything in the world exists in order to end up as an opera. An opera without music is what we call everyday life. Poetry is opera without the story, score, costumes, make-up, or staging. It's a libretto set to its own music. The reader is both the conductor and lead singer. The audience gathers at the unconscious. Tickets are sold only on the morning of the performance; students pay half but often stand. Unsatisfied customers may claim refunds for twice the cost of admission; these are paid directly by the poet.

"You've got a lot of moxie."

The "double silly" consists of making two complete turns with another person while walking in the street.

I've got my next few years of work mapped out for me: figuring out what to do over the next few years.

When you say baroque you're barking up the wrong tree, which suits me.

The station wagon stayed stationary at the station.

Stunned he put down his gun and started to run.

The Jew stops being the Jew when the movie's over.

No horizon on the horizon.

Going to sleep to continue the story.

Third eye hindsighted.

Making another patch for the patch.

There's no business like no business like no business I know.

Blue is no longer blue when it loses its hue.

Terrible day to start the way. (Terrible way to start to stray.)

If language could talk we would refuse to understand it.

Hue is a property of optics not objects.

As to "avant garde": I am not in advance of anything but perhaps close, in the neighborhood, around.

Better to come up from behind than to lead. If you lead you'd have to know where you are going whereas I only know where I am not going.

The politics in a poem has to do with how it enters the world, how it makes its meaning, how its forms work in social contexts. The politics in a poem is specific to poetry not politics.

Now I am getting weary of ideology and would like to give it up entirely but it seems the more I give it up the more it has me by the throat. I write so I can breathe.

And better artificial respiration than no respiration. Better imaging reparation than silence.

Or let's say trying to re-imagine the possibilities of sentience through the material sentience of language.

Don't ask me to be frank. I don't even know if I can be myself.

You never know what invention will look like or else it wouldn't be invention.

We see each other as if with hidden sensors. Those not tuned in miss the action entirely, even when it's right before their eyes.

The Greeks had an idea of *nostos*, which is not quire what we call nostalgia. *Nostos* suggests the political and ethical responsibility of the human being in orienting herself or himself. You can't go home again but you can stay tuned to your senses of responsibility.

So much depends upon what you are expecting.

The chicken she is cooked but the liver is raw.

As for we who love to be admonished . . .

Certain that this satin would intoxicate even Satan; the trips of the trade, the lisps of the frayed.

If that's the price I will pay it but not gladly.

Like I told her, you can add up all the zeros in the world but it will never amount to anything. Whereas two plus two, while barely four, suggests progress.

If progress is a process, what is the purpose of purpose or the allure of allure?

You see I told you so but you weren't listening or maybe I forgot to press SEND.

It is equally problematic to shout "Theater!" at a crowded fire.

I break for speed bumps.

Eugene Ormandy wore organdy. George Solti speaks in sotto voce. Toscanini dons a bikini. Neville Marriner slides down the banister. Herbert von Karajan had two carry-ons. Kurt Masur abhors clamor.

Everything that happens in life exists to be reflected on in Boca.

"Do you see that? Those people came in after us and they're being served first."

It takes a village to read a poem.

The patter of petunias in the marmalade.

Everybody's got to be somewhere.

Save the last chance for me.

from *Michigan Quarterly Review*

Token Enabler

◊   ◊   ◊

forced to cuddle but some heirloom of power and peril it must be
I have sufferings natural to me and a desire to repeat the clear truth

let me out of here—plunder and I, we hawk light to random passers-by
brutal on our own time sweet phantasm's inner thigh kisses back

fully equipped token enabler glazed anxiety picks feathers under wings
with stunted emotions to shriek freely about the dollars for space do call

contracts are meant to be signed then read wake up and check birdy's collar
has he chewed through it? opened up his back? give vet hundreds for another

chew toy blood test rapid cycling on the window sill wracked by construction
but he still loves he doesn't know the syringe full of nasty-ass meds

is for his calamity he just knows I'm gonna jam it into his beak traced out
loophole to intelligence stations' mayday flood the hull with fuel and detonate

when sick o write a poem you take care of me trapped things with power we be
androgyne vs. cyborg drapes this event outside the body box I owe you

a working clash conscience piggy scrape something scabbed off your and my
        backs
repeat ten thousand times a day: self-mutilation a poetics when I feel fine in
        place

I know I'm fucked by soft thoughts green panda blankies clear band-aids
wireless craniums spread silence rations 'twas friendly in caves a pity

about those emotions getting in the way of rational resistance to The Fury
  stacked
upside down on the citizenry I'm said to be in contempt of a wiser love
  should I

write your vows? Whenever I know how to spill my guts all over the polemic
lifetime original drooling in a network's daring choice of subjection no one

knows what happens when giant squids mate world authorities yearn to witness
beacon suckers emerge while subject to a harsh environmental variable sur-
  rounding

object flesh panel by panel legit as flow and just enough clothes and shit to
  present
a virus comes and considers going I see my person every morning and it ain't
  me

and I like it that way with song and difficulty taking the opportunity to take care
of us as total time to spend no dumping get your health forms into the right slot

I know in my experience at work my problem is not my communication
skills it's the fact that I'm communicating to the wrong people

from *Rattapallax, Mississippi Review,*
and *Can We Have Our Ball Back?*

from *Blasted Fields of Clover*
Bring Harrowing and Regretful Sighs

◊　◊　◊

Now the sea moves up the lawn for him as those nearby view his life passing before their eyes. Someone his own age lean in black pants and a white shirt sits on a plastic chair with a block of massive green light. Facing of someone else away (bluebird). This is not happening to him. Unaccountable ejaculation. Briefs halted at the knees alter his walk. The basement conceals a surplus of chairs while overground the yards remain square and trimmed to uniform length (clouds). This was written on his arm. Its words occupy a grid and move among cells at random with great speed. A car leaves a driveway and exclamations are made about wood left over and what could make it burn.

. . .

Stacked circles (rain down) say green it releases nothing. Bundled wires. Ellsworth Kelly strides from one red iceberg to the next. Each face projects onto antennae forging a domain expressed as a skewered pod. Transparency behind a desk elusive plunge. A dissection of thought into its components the weight of meat up the wrong street the wrong backdoor. The blazer missed too as the wiry one observed. Someone slipped him diet Orangina and he went ballistic. The whole staff crayoned their names onto the good luck card while unwitting partygoers waited for the elevator. Mogul and musician separated at birth one suggested. Hubris. The directions very specific and yet so many stood idle. She ravished in black. He charmed in lime.

from *Boston Review*

The Walk

◇ ◇ ◇

The woman came toward me through the woods with a hatchet.
She was coming through the woods with a shotgun.
The trees bent and swayed around the path,

a delicate canopy, the lake a dropped quarter behind
the brink. And the near-mute lap, tendril lick,

was it the lake—or lacy wings of butterflies leaping
from leaves? Oh, the least of these. She, brisk
with bullet holes, carrying a butcher knife.

"From those who have nothing, even what they have
will be taken away," I thought, as she walked tugging her examination gloves,

stainless steel stethoscope around her shot-through throat.
"For to all those who have, more will be given,"
I said aloud as she strode toward me in her leotard

and rapped thrice on my head with a cloth-covered brick.
I heard her count through the hole in her throat,

raspy as the crow-cackle grating from their roost
in the tall dead tree which moaned and creaked as it bent side-stitched,
its shriveled roots spread miles under the earth, miles to the water table

where the red and eyeless millipedes prune their poison sacs,
and outward wide as the woods where the mushroom hunters

hunt in the moist dew dawns. (She had me by a cord around my throat.
She had me in the net-and-pulley treetrap.) "Oh, to the least, to me,"
I wheezed, and pointed out the sun, still high in the sky, still spotted

with sun spots. I took her spotted hand in mine as we both looked up into
        the blue,
and the long honey locust pods rattled high in the honey locust tree.

from *Conduit*

MICHAEL BURKARD

a cloud of dusk

◊　◊　◊

i can't see anymore
i missed every Memphis angel
because of the because clauses—
one night sleeping with two cats
Big and Little
and i am serious about these names
i had a vision reading a John Irving book
i did not want to read never presumed i would read
more than a few pages
there were hallway lights and people's voices
shivering through a downstairs window
i could not put the book down either
even though i literally wanted to put it down
sometimes—i hate that word—i went to a meeting
nearby and i was accidentally or coincidentally on this street
so much i began to think maybe i belong here
i kissed the back of someone's hand
i kissed the hand when it turned back to me
i made sure no page was facing me when i read
and that no one would see what i saw or feel what i felt
i am on a drive where a mirror has collapsed
i want to ask someone else without sight

from *Lyric*

Gnosticism

◇   ◇   ◇

I

Heaven's lips! I dreamed
of a page in a book containing the word "bird" and I
entered "bird."
Bird grinds on,

grinds on, thrusting against black. Thrusting
wings, thrusting again, hard
banks slap against it either side, that bird was exhausted.

Still, beating, working its way and below in dark woods
small creatures
leap. Rip

at food with scrawny lips.
Lips at night.
Nothing guiding it, bird beats on, night wetness on it.
A lion looks up.
Smell of adolescence in these creatures, this ordinary
night for them. Astonishment

inside me like a separate person,
sweat-soaked. How to grip.
For some people a bird sings, feathers shine. I just get this *this*.

II

Forgot? how the mind goes at it, you open
the window (late), there is a siffling sound,
that cold smell before sleep, roofs,
frozen staircase, frozen stair,
a piece of it comes in.

Comes in, stands in the room a bit of a column of it alive.
At first no difference, then palely, a dust,
an indentation, stain
of some guest
centuries ago.

Some guest *at this very hour,* was it final love or the usual
I said! you said! oh, the body,
no listen, unpinning itself, slam of car door,
snow. Far, far, far, far.

Washed in the blood of that.

III

First line has to make your brain race that's how Homer does it,
that's how Frank O'Hara does it, why
at such a pace
Muses
slam through the house—there goes one (fainting) up the rungs
of your strange BULLFIGHT, buttered
almost in a nearness
to skyblue
Thy pang—Pollock yourself!
Just to hang onto life is why

IV

*They found the dog! Mother died! He didn't mean to hang up just
a bad connection! No time for lipstick if I answer that but isn't
there a Ladies' outside Philosophy anyway they never start
till ten after oh rats now I've lost the Gertrude Stein
quote was it beefsteak?*—what

swarm of clearnesses and do they amaze you,
inbetween when you hear the phone and when you get it,
all palpable explanations of why it rang and what to do
and what'd it be like if your brain were this fit
all the time? Say,

at the moment in the interminable dinner when Coetzee basking
icily across from you at the faculty table is all at once
there like a fox in a glare, asking
And what are your interests?
his face a glass that has shattered but not yet fallen.

V

". . . what the little word *after* means . . ."
(I. Kant, *Inaugural Dissertation* 2.399.4–6)

Stuffed September night, the hot leaves bump
on swollen breezes and a fat
black moonlessness.
I got up (3 a.m.)

to clean the house, there was
so much pressure on it forcing the butt end down.
I scrubbed counters and mopped floors.
I didn't turn the lights on.
Cleaning

in the dark makes a surprise for later. By then
I will have
slept, woke, come striding back

from infuriated interiors—ah
now

recall
I dreamed
of Wordsworth—his little vials,
Wordsworth collected little vials,
had hundreds of them, his sister stored them on shelves in the pantry—
and yes

to inspire me is why
I put in a bit of Wordsworth but then the page is over, he weighs it to the
          ground,
the autumn of him soaking my mop purple in the dyes of what's falling
breathless under its own
senses.

VI

Walking the wild mountain in a storm I saw the great trees throw their
          arms.
Ruin! they cried and seemed aware

the sublime is called a "science of anxiety."
What do men and women know of it?—at first

not even realizing they were naked!
The language knew.

Watch "naked" (*arumim*) flesh slide into "cunning" (*arum*) snake in the next
          verse.
And suddenly a vacancy, a silence,

is somewhere inside the machine.
Veins pounding.

from *The New Yorker*

Landscape with a Calm

(from a painting by Poussin)

◊   ◊   ◊

The man with the goats has seen this light before.
He enjoys it, takes it seriously, but does not turn on his heel
To get a better view. His dog awaits instructions.
People like him have stepped into the same river twice.

I grant you (imagine this barked by a Labrador) that blues and yellows
Sometimes turn things aside from the way they are normally.
For instance, the grass on the low escarpment by the south approach
Is pulled sideways by the sun most afternoons, as if good grazing
Could go on forever, like lava or glacier ice, but cooling, slowing,
Green as grass, maybe, but grass mashed by a pumice
Into an eternal dry paste. Epidermis, cosmetic,
Shadow on the eyes of a face.

The two women in the windows of the high castle
Could care less about green. The world comes to them
Essentially as sound, warmth, a flooding of low energies into oddly
          shaped receptacles.
Bagpipe music (finally tolerable). Birch leaves. The smell of stubble fires
          being doused.

Don't assume that men on galloping horses are in a hurry.

It's the same old story (the stock figure speaks up). Goats do not take a lot
          of managing,
The dog is underemployed fifty percent of the time,
But there are always sufficient local shenanigans for us

To be on the wrong side of the river when the sun goes down.
Numbers of times I have measured the last mile and a half
Against the inclination of shadow on the washhouse roof
And decided not.

I do not believe that aromas, even of ash, can be therapy
Any more than the bust in the innermost room of the castle, *onyx,*
      émail—
Waiting for the dark ages, offering them its Roman nose.
Art is not a set of survival skills. The city in the water
Is enough of a stereotype, the city on the hill having failed us.

To be specific, look at the sky. Not the same blue everywhere
But not changeable, not empty, not the blue of a house by the sea.
Not a philosopher's thinking away of particulars,
Or a painter's pressing the flesh and having ether be up front;
Sky blue, but sky seemingly touched by something not of this world,
A brush or a glove, until it looks the same way for a week.

from *The Threepenny Review*

The Centrifuge

◊   ◊   ◊

It is difficult to describe what we felt
after we had paid the admission,
entered the aluminum dome,

and stood there with our mouths open
before the machine itself,
what we had only read about in the papers.

Huge and glistening it was
but bolted down and giving nothing away.

What did it mean?
we all wondered openly,
and did another machine exist somewhere—
an even mightier one—
that was designed to be its exact opposite?

These were not new questions,
but we asked them earnestly and repeatedly.

And later when we were home again—
a family of six having tea—
we raised these questions once more,
knowing that this made us part
of a great historical discussion
that included science
as well as literature and the weather

not to mention the lodger downstairs,
who, someone said,
had been seen earlier leaving the house
with a suitcase and a tightly furled umbrella.

from *Fulcrum*

3-4-00

◊   ◊   ◊

Sundown
at Walden Pond. Redwings
singing, plump Canadas
all around.

"Whew!"
say the starlings. Song-sparrow
song breaks into
delicacies I've never heard before.

Meadowlark whistling
on pink smear
below three pictures:
pasture, pits and refuge.

Sun descending
somewhere south of James.
Hooded merganser
swimming near the far (north) shore.

Jet trails
like 'live scars;
something's
happening up there.

Sewage domes as ever
silver the north edge. Long's
peeks over—robin
warble.

Plane and glider . . .
everything turns blue
and I wonder again
who's pushing who?

from *Ecopoetics*

MICHAEL COSTELLO

Ode to My Flint and Boom Bolivia

◊ ◊ ◊

seems to me I have   & am thankful
for the complete sets   of limericks and sensory topics
facsimiles—though they don't work so well—
earmarks   tools & my unique-to-me covering
of skylarks   I am also grateful   for you minimum
bramble   two lockets   hemstitch   or other lack
for that special maverick   encased by the skylight
which brings me to booms   connected to a few
more   constructing the skepticism which hasn't
let me down—too much as of now—& has had
a smooth run with time   & on a few occasions has
been put to the tetanus   & accelerated

so far luster   you still fuse   so the divisors tell me
but you don't fester   like you did   once I remember
being able to sabotage forever   & ripple a billboard
for milk   & plod to the basilica   which I was
sonorous about   the fact that sleights of hand wouldn't
give me lightning enough to drum—always a dream—
before pumping sludge   into you (it)   in myriad ways

Bolivia   I apologize   do you   Pandora   whose fault
are you   a rebel free radical   wasting unknown
demimondes   wasting this skylight   to know the importance
of your role   played & playing & now   I can never forget
you—your negligence constantly reminds—

nevertheless   thank you   all of you   unmentioned troops
in the Bloody Mary   cedar & musicale   & elsewhere
we've come a long way—in fact though   none of you are
the originals   are you   you are the great grandchildren etc.
of the original hearthstone   llama   luster   stoop   skylarks
half-life   artifice   spiral   stigma   et al.—thank you   I celebrate
and show you always   today   to the morning sum   & nightly
sway you   in commitments   & commemorate you   with comets
I am my Bolivia's keeper   & it is mine   & seems thus far
it has been a beneficial religion   for all passengers involved
and so then   let my Bolivia keep on

from *Columbia Poetry Review*

MICHAEL DAVIDSON

Bad Modernism

◊ ◊ ◊

Suddenly all is / loathing
—John Ashbery

and there's plenty to be unhappy about
if I can just get the reception area festooned
in time for their arrival, paper cups
and those little plastic whatsits so that,
gorged on meaning,
they troop through the glass doors
seeking interpretation, first floor
mildly historical, second floor
desire matrix, parents accompany
their indiscretions straight
to the penthouse, and someone
hands them a phone, "turtles"
they're call led, heads bobbing
as though they had a choice
to be party favors, deep structure
on your left follow the clicking
to a white cube, we only work
part time, the other part
we illustrate profound malaise,
I like these cream-filled versions
so unlike what we get at home,
having said which
we re-wind the tape,
slip it through a slot marked "aha"
and take the E home,

the smell you smell afar
is something boiling over.

from *No: a journal of the arts*

You Art A Scholar, Horatio, Speak To It

◇ ◇ ◇

You say you walk and sew alone?
I walk and sew alone.

You say you gape and waver?
I am mostly dizzy, most open-mouthed.

You say you taste it with each dish?
I drink it and I spit it up.

You say it lays you face-down?
I kiss the dirt.

Carved into your bone china?
Mine's more fine.

Folded into your laundry?
Dry. Dry. Dry.

Is it quite awful and unbearable?
Quite.

Is it sweet and gentle?
Most sweet, most gentle.

Does it make you retch?
I am wretched.

Do you write it poems?
I compose on it daily.

Is it epic?
In thought and in treatment.

Do you cry upon it?
It is flat and wet.

Will you humor it?
Forever.

Will you forsake it?
Never.

You say you keep it in a box?
I've Cornelled mine.

You say you call it soft names?
I call it softly. I name it.

Clipped of fledge?
Clipped of fledge.

You say it sits up on your soul?
It has it licked.

A new religion?
Nay, a faith.

Do you take it to bed?
I've pillowed and I've laid with it.

Does it propagate?
I sharpen my chastity upon it.

I belt it. I go down on it.
I keep it down.

Have you done your best to bury it?
I have dug.

With half a heart?
With dull spade, yea, half-heartedly.

Has it a sword?
A long-tailed lion on its crest.

Would you unknow it?
I've called it bastard.

Bastard!
Would you divorce it?

Untie it, would you?
Have you

Done with it?
No. I will have more.

from *Tin House*

Prose of the World Order

◇   ◇   ◇

This blue
is nothing but elastic
sound everlasting a relapse
improbable neither vegetable
nor animal
not even personal but
sonorous as lexical hash
hypothetically
a novella by a fellow guest here
left finally dead
as matter might
stick to a wall
virgin in shape or exquisitely
scrawled
the gist of which is
We exist in places
otherwise strange and probably
impassible.
Yet here
yours is not the first face
to appear
surrounded upright
on two feet awake
stunned from the sleep of a Nobody

Curiously peering
into an icon of yourself
captive in a cubicle
(nice spot to adapt to

maybe
after channeling Emerson).
Some of us lack the luxury
of being nowhere
unaccountable
hence our methodism
(divine or boredom?)
and our jobs.
Scrip floats up for grabs
spun from thin air
for us gilded free
from the company
flywheels
of a motorized chair
slow boat from here
to there long since
locked away like a young
onion in the silt
shade of deferred and elegant
oaks standing
standing still standing
radiant
as dialectical ballast
to this alchemical
mixing of apparent opposites
gold and gas
first and last ecstaticle
motivating hillwise
as we ply broad day
light I say
its instants under plain
square sky
unreconstructed and leaving
behind us
in our exodus
our old Gestetner
booming
iambic as a house
gusseted to plackets in the hard
slippage

we'll always be known by
into the new

Solitude of a motor park.
Blue days equal almost salty
ones in the perpetuity of sight
seeing
whose sphincter clings
to a fleck overcome
with personality fluttering
naively perfect through sleep
where dialectical ballast is
the picture itself
and the prose of its obverse or
curses foiled when shove
comes to push
the mud of the flood
up to a door
like a hatch in the present
of absent disarticulation
strewn with little joints
of party mix; it's how we get
along (self-
selection) gently letting neighbors
know you're one of those
animals
endowed with speech *or* one of those who
listens. Plaid-suited
between the glorious lines
of the seven species of talk
(horizontal, uniform, and swimming)
my eyes have seen the coming
of our internal works by day
dropping the pretense when night
falls on all
six of us who call ourselves "I"
without abandon

And for how long?
You may be a cousin

twice removed from town
down alone in Shadow Valley
or so your tag suggests
just as someone else begins to whistle
Jenny Can't Sit Still
then commences
hanging out Old Warbler's rags
on sticks. The pastoral *it*
(yesterday's abjection
in today's machine)
was being reamed
by a contraption; all I know
is what the words know and the long
sonata for Nobody and
her ingot of a blue
tongue
(inexplicably thick
it seemed the spine of someone
else inside her
more metal than meter
meter than memory
and ticked).
Would she have anywhere to go but west
to east
to some unspeakably hackneyed
medical destination a depot
a desk from which
to contemplate the original definition of *sunset*
as financially secure?

The plaid animal thought not
furiously cribbing from notes
but willing then
to reset the counter at zero again
late as it was and ruined
with finger trouble. A claim
a double dose a middle a hose
make themselves friendly
to any living that wants to go
in (—fate

of any figure
in a picture). But what is
inside her except another brave scene
another burnt-out
antechamber—longer
paler . . . ? The plosive stream
smoothes out again
corrupted only by the failure
of dull correctives. Remember
Nobody's tongue?
When it shows up wet
will you stand flat?
Bother to call it Mother?
Rear up like a horse
to the original slap
of retraction? The sound
of which (appeal
wail—at last
a form of speech)
brings all the gold of the sky to bear
as particles of time
massed along the border
lane in nothing
fine
but a fly in the ardor of precision

from *26: A Journal of Poetry and Poetics*

13

◇　◇　◇

You are often hunched over in an armchair to confide sweet nothings to the side of a face. In this sense, you resemble a bassoon. Though you expect the most extravagant praises for the most trivial accomplishments, you shun and despise those who view you favorably.

As sunlight slants down on another late afternoon, you are strumming on a guitar, eating shepherd's pie, and sipping rum-laced coffee. Always bitterly exuberant, you see life as a pink spathe swathing a yellow spadix. Tonight, standing in a musty hallway, you will speak your penultimate line with some dignity.

You are often seen in profile at the top of a stairs, listening to a distant music. Your hair is bouffant in the front, flat in the back. Your best view is three-quarter. A minute or two after midnight, champagne will spill from your fragrant mouth.

As you bend down to retrieve a long-lost favor, someone seizes you by the shoulder. You are such a master at aestheticizing your crimes that even your victims are grateful to be included in the horrible photographs.

Inducing doubt and self-hatred in all those you come into contact with, you are a cancer and a pig. When a stream of your indulgent reveries is nixed by an unpleasant, ghastly image, you let out a high C and touch yourself immodestly.

"A straight line is easy enough," you hear in a dream, "but it is not possible to draw a perfect circle." You smirk at this provocation. Waking up, you work all night on an endless piece of paper, drawing circle after circle, each one wobbly, obloid, squarish, rectangular, some are outright triangles.

Trying to peel away your fingers, someone pleads, "Let go of me!" but you are already beyond discretion. Like every other human being, you crave a single moment of absolute exposure. Today will be your day. Your veins will pop out.

Overhearing, "Where I come from, people don't . . ." you punch the speaker, a blind, elderly immigrant, in the face, knocking two teeth out, before you yourself are knocked unconscious by a blunt instrument from behind. Waking up days later, you are told by a lugubrious dog that he, too, has often slept through the best parts.

In the men's room of a small town bus terminal, you discover your oil portrait in a trash can. You cut the canvas out, then stuff your folded face into your back pocket. Later, you notice with irritation that where your nose should be is a clay pipe, and your mouth is just a hole.

You cannot understand the story of a youth who falls in love with his own reflection in a spring. Where you are, water does not reflect. Nothing reflects. One's view of oneself is made up entirely of other people's verbal slanders.

Told by your employer to buy a new shirt, you respond, "To buy a new shirt is to assume that I have at least two more years to live. Such presumptuousness cannot go unpunished. What's more, there would be this outlandish incongruity between a brand-new shirt and my already worn-out body. Such an incongruity would cause my entire being, every single cell, to feel an unspeakable shame, a shame not on the skin, but in the skin, a shame to bring on my early death."

You wake up to a jungly tune. On the ceiling is a water stain showing your mother's face in three-quarter view. A suspicious fluid drips on your forehead. You wish there were a hand the size of an umbrella to protect you from all this fresh degradation.

from *American Poetry Review*

RITA DOVE

All Souls'

◇ ◇ ◇

Starting up behind them,
all the voices of those they had named:
mink, gander, and marmoset,
crow and cockatiel.
Even the duck-billed platypus,
of late so quiet in its bed,
sent out a feeble cry signifying
grief and confusion, et cetera.

Of course the world had changed
for good. As it would from now on
every day, with every twitch and blink.
Now that change was de rigueur,
man would discover desire, then yearn
for what he would learn to call
distraction. This was the true loss.
And yet in that first

unchanging instant,
the two souls
standing outside the gates
(no more than a break in the hedge;
how had they missed it?) were not
thinking. Already the din was fading.
Before them, a silence
larger than all their ignorance

yawned, and this they walked into
until it was all they knew. In time

they hunkered down to business,
filling the world with sighs—
these anonymous, pompous creatures,
heads tilted as if straining
to make out the words to a song
played long ago, in a foreign land.

from *The New Yorker*

Draft 55: Quiptych

◇   ◇   ◇

> *The most beautiful order of the world*
> *is still a random gathering of things*
> *insignificant of themselves.*
> —Herakleitos

There had been the logos. A long long time ago,
seasoned with châteaux. That quip was worth it?
"The scene opens" again. It opens differently.
Indifferently. Deliciously. At random. As for rule:

"There are two things, a dictionary and the country."
I could follow that logic, if not perfectly.
They're any labyrinth of words or things,
both the intimate spaces of singular being

and drawn out notions on a quartered screen
quadru-puling experience. Dailiness folds
its riddle over, tears astonishment in half
and half again, insignificant fragments

pointedly one's own. Scraps re-collected
in tranquiddity, suggestive and distressed.
The paper, words, and statements torn to specks
are watered well with "tears," pronounced as best

"to melt" the paper down and not, this time, "to rip."
All soupy, slosh and pulp, soaked and stirred,
the shredded porridge then gets scooped,
netted in deckle, sprung, and hung to dry.

This pre-book liquidated or solidified,
messages scumbled, agitated, effaced,
words melted down, unread, erased,
the former letters pressed as blankness

into paper. Then after, crotcheted into quartos.
New-made paper having thereupon been written
gets named page: an original awkward as its translation,
a translation riffling ceaselessly through idioms.

Today was the night of the day War started again.
I want history told as transition between dream
and waking, my random dream, the cultural dream.
Of course I'm interested in "the essay as from."

My eye core split and doubled. I picked the duck out;
also distinguished rabbit. And that was just the start.
They fellowed me with other beasts and birds besides,
down dark word roads you've heard about before,

irregularly blazed by dictionary or as country.
The political air is clotted and runny.
Though Herakleitos spoke of matter without history,
it's hardly possible. "I have" a buggy landscape,

"I have" a national space: its mine-field coup,
its choiceless manipulation, obliviously wrecked,
stuffed with obesities of things
and stroke-drunk stunned by pointed threats.

I open the dictionary in random curiosity
and studious struggle, scratching at my sweaty
thoughts under this traditional, handmade paper hat.
I want the unsayable twice and twice again;

I want a different dictionary. (And a different country.)
Did words I chose exist or not? Can I even spell?
The Dictionary names Things in this particular Country.
But native bugs want neither etymology

nor entomology, though they know their own needs—
a parallel world, another knowledge of the country.
Equipped with four lines at a go, quaternion,
Words and their vectoring Governance I work—

not the definitional geography of Passports
(mine easily stamped; this easy to say),
but rather striations and cross-fertilizations
of mixy, murky middens titled "word play."

Would I claim to "legislate" another government?
I can't even get the one I want the normal (voting) way.
At odds in the uneven world, an unsettled settler,
I therefore admire "the essay as from." From what?

We all served a term apprenticed to beauty
but stopped when "heroes" for this tale emerged
as motes blown here and there, as pulpy scraps,
as "N" (na na nahh) or "Y" (ya ya yehh).

So there. But didn't mean it quite that way;
it just came out in that flip tone.
Tauntingly. As if to prove the Book of Words
does not encompass all the langues one knows.

Fit my whole life sifting through
one conjuncture of mud and grit
in an era of shame, sitting shiva
at a saturated crossroads under cloud,

shivering as heavy rains come down,
alphabets blown at my head, prior to definition.
Squalling gray, the letters hit in drops
lit greenly uncannily cold and blur.

This is the so-called "falling rain texture"
of "true-view" style, where loss is palpable,
fantastic rocks, blankness and misty water,
invisible scenes and attenuated syntaxes.

No longer fluent in loveliness for l'anguish,
there is another language back of the language.
I hear it, it drones, it keens pebbling,
pooling. Draws out this well so clear and crisp

a shimmered, watery draft, unquenchable,
that feeds a thirst impossible to sense
one even had, but had to drink from it,
sipping itself on the edge of the edge.

There is no Dictionary for this gathering,
these folds of words, their floods, their flares,
their turns, their bonds. Shadows cast full sorts.
A shopping bag tears and newspapers spill out

layering lies, scattering rues and trues
under suspect motives, over intransigent confusion.
Manipulated—this   Killed—that
stippled with suffering and collusion.

For the world is burning with money
and resonant with outrage.
Ordinary, has dark bleeding.
Transfixed by this news

its heartless calculation, its profound sadness.
Then (really) saw a hedgehog drinking at a puddle.
Wild sights! wild sights!
"I wake up every morning haunted."

Thus everything folds over everything else.
No matter what it is, it pivots and crumples;
auras of both words and things fall in
upon themselves. The poem is a multiple fold

for carrying on this quirky, painful trip,
a quiptych set up neatly on a slate-flat rock,
or on the bureau of a brown hotel;
but even at home in the little light of day

one takes a dazzling journey every turn,
even waiting in an airport and wishing
one's modicum of wishes in that in-between,
the poem offers a multiple fold for carrying.

No climax. A grid, a quip, a contour map, from where,
with paper folded so, you see a section of the country.
"I would like very much to stay longer in the country."
Something like, but in what country?

This is what: we shine about, we hinge
carefully, open the panels, light and dark
and fragments, caught mid-tunnel half a mile from
either end, among the ark of random things.

—June–August 2002, Umbria
to Peter Quartermain

from *Conjunctions*

Notes

Draft 55: Quiptych. The source of the epigraph is Guy Davenport, trans., Herakleitos, cited by Peter Quartermain, *Disjunctive Poetics*, 168. "There are two things, a dictionary and the country" and "I would like very much to stay longer in the country" were said by Gertrude Stein in "Saving the Sentence," *How to Write* [1931] (New York: Dover Publications, 1975), 19 and 17. The traditional handmade paper hat, in fact, was worn by typesetters. History to contain dream elements is based on something said by Walter Benjamin, *The Arcades Project*, 464, which I decided to take literally, not figuratively, as humanity waking up from dream into history. "Essay as from" is a typo in a book on Theodor Adorno. "If you are caught mid-tunnel half mile from either end, 'basically you kiss yourself goodbye,' the man said." Frank Ortiz, cited from an article written by Randy Kennedy about tunnel workers, *New York Times*, November 20, 2001, metro section, D3. Donor drafts are Draft 17: Unnamed and Draft 36: Cento.

short sorry

◊   ◊   ◊

"Now," or never or can't be . . . "this question," now that "was easy,"
maybe two easys for the price of one. I remember when it wasn't the
other day and there was someone over there, right on that spot, it was
one of those lead moments, "a day in the life" or written as if an owner's
manual. "Built for," constructed by, anD here to serve the ones we
love, "obvious members of," but the wrong. number. 'is this . . . ?' 'no
and don't you ever call again,' or it was the right number in reverse; 27.4
million pounds of distorted meat, instead of destroyed meat, in reverse,
"considering the Order," which was arbitrary, is arbitrary, must be arbi-
trary, and completely . without any proper neckware, but a call to order,
please, "of the Tribe of Elevation." with a cleaver and a gnat of verbs we
mount the block-Print and, "As it was considered an under-score,"
drove the rest into the lot-o-mirth, . . . glory be to the hell-hall and may
the mighty spirit of groucho marx prevent us from a repeat syntax
armageddon . . . "of The Good Life Society Ltd." to have existed some-
where, just about here, not long after the other ones came and left, claim-
ing to have invented the 4' 33" of silence, long before the john cage
fraternal order came to own all silence. "AD." "and I" and before that
"came" esp., et al's and fac that we are . cond col of the crt so nb the gigo
dacrim cpiauxbf mfa's and tgif . . . Lt's who frEq frwy's and fx env's "to
grip" "s"t "wit" here to and "it." "Wit." wit or without it, "It was some-
thing fit for" a bit-o dinner for four or a chicken pot pie make for "the
clan's voodoo hoodoo," after . . . "of" "which the four Horseless," all taxi
drivers stood and looked . . at all the "Wonders." "As" if one was the
other's assumption which "they opposed" as an anything to do w/ the
answer 'all of the above-or none of the rest.' so, the lords, and ladies of
the near . east end stopped doing drag_ and became other people's . .
people. and sat and wondered "of the Comet and" other parts. "the fall"

came much much later, "of"ten as a reminder of "the empire." stokes out pArt 50.

"I came to grips." at around age ten or so, maybe a line of a different order, it was during the moon landing "& messiness was understood" as something dirty, something you only do if you are sick and caught in deep clots of blood "as almost important" as the rEal answer. "The answer" to my future blindness should have been foretold not by tea leaves sent "to the Brigadier" of family matters, and "Everlasting." demigod on my block, but by the hair on my hand. "The House" was silent. as I wouLd show up for dinner and try to hide my hands and have trouble opening the cans "of Armore" condolence ham. or the time we all went to "The King of" burgers and every one stared as I put mustard on my thing, it was as if I was king "Kong Co-op" of all mimes, waiting for fay wray. "The / same / way" I got help when on special days "the letter" of all letters "arrives and we" or I, depends on the moment "opened them" it depends on the Moment, and "almost" as I could "quickly" say; 'sei nicht so grausam, bleib.' something else was to happen as "though I admit" now how "quickly" it "sounded like": 'fuhrt mich nich in versuchung . . .' I meant get the "quicksilver" tooth brush "and our" souls will be saved. at that moment "bikes fell," I jumped. "apart" from the rest. "quite easily" I might add. "This was the question" I had "alluDed to. It was" as "easy" as nichts . .

from *Aufgabe*

Sibling Rivalry

◇　◇　◇

I

Home after home after home.
What's to become of us
two separatist homebodies?

Home away from home, cliffside,
awaiting apocalyptic landslide rumble.
Clocktower of regimented girlie-boys,
cutesy-wootsy samba every hour on the hour,
their whirligig shadows elongated on the moat.
Swirled away in a flashflood, adulthood toppled.

Yah yah, us foundlings were riven,
amen, by infantile body parts.
My hernia scar emitted air raid siren screeches.
Doctor Caligari grotesqueries
rife with phantom pain mayhem,
a high maintenance cornucopia
shriven by braindrain panic-induced.

Nya nya nya, what a to-do. What to do.
Entertain the troops with ritzy kitschy improvs,
cross-eyed Heils, or melt into the crowd,
muttering imprecations at scuffed ebony parquets,
stomped on by hup-two vigilantes.

Abandoned in a rice paddy rivulet, in extremis,
end of term, my war years are a blank.
Cromwell. Rommel. Fraulein Zaza, gaga,
"wannabe twee pixie strung up on a fambly teepee"
so her sloe-eyed vamp whiskey voice croaketh,
Candygram hand-delivered
QUINTS ALIVE AND WELL

II

Counterfeit samenesses in virtual reality center my innards. I might add,
git no kick from Kitchen Sink Verismo. Lemme explain. If besmirched
by puberty influx smut—gravitas is insufficient. I'd ice up in a void if I
didn't macerate with kith. Counterfeit samenesses in virtual reality
center my innards. Witch. Childhood. She made curtains flurry, pokin'
her haid through my bedroom window. Senior citizens had best skirt
the harrowing vagaries of long-term memory retrieval. *I* do. Counter-
feit samenesses in virtual reality center my innards. Porn classics with
simplistic sound bytes—howls and yowls, infinity in a rush seem dif-
ferent every Re-re-re-re-re-repeat. The Reveal in the Barracks. Rainbow
prisms. Jissom prisms. Counterfeit samenesses in virtual reality center
my innards.

III

Meanwhile, pre-glass-bottom boats,
back at the asylum, pre-caravanserai,
quality folks, abed in attic cul-de-sacs,
glared up at Louis Quinze meathooks.
Kin, via shock treatment spasms,
shat out conversation pit sputum.

IV

Back at the safari,
precursor stalwarts reeled in salmon,
shot pampas zebras, fjord hippos,
wham, went blind.

Daydreams in steamrooms.
Nance fantasies. Gung-ho lunges
at tent show sleaze, lowlife lures.
Slouchy cowboys. Sailor crotches.
The bump and grind of silhouette sex.

V

First home away from home
I piled up itchy bales of ranch alfalfa—
Favela Hovel for Tyke Couchant,
disrupter of garden plenitude:
irrigated rosebeds, jungle gym swings,
rabbits cosseted with fresh cage straw,
round swimming pool kept bereft
of dead weeping willow leaves.
A surround of tall trees muffled car skids,
black chow yaps, freight train hullabaloo.

VI

The Garden of the Gods
taught me vertigo high up—
red sandstone hulks,
a two-hump camel.

Sahara-dry prairie sheared
by blue Rockies, wavery sky wall
capped by snow all summer long.
I spun in a flux of distance dread.

Pikes Peak. Pikes Peak.
    Pining for Pikes Peak.
Unfindable Pikes Peak.

VII

The outside world,
The endlessness of its endlessness.
Lost Empires to map.
Inca. Aztec. Codes to crack.
Toy cars. Oz. War. Afar.
My very own Princess, Margaret Rose.
Adolf Hitler's radio rant.
My very own Empire under attack.
Cooled ear pressed
against sprinkled on grass,
if I listened hard, past its crust,
through Planet Earth's
molten lava core,
from my safe perch
I heard China roar.

from *New American Writing*

337,000, December, 2000

◊   ◊   ◊

1.

They are formidable, the wild geese, in their numbers.
They lie down in the rushes and become reeds.
The leaf-shaped facts, in fact, have many shapes.

Use reuses itself to become design—
The sketcher's brushstroke determines the count and the light
And how it is absorbed and at what angles.

The beak that widened to meet the prey,
The cry a half-tone higher.

Literature is an infiltration of the mind
By its stops. The mandarins stopped to wonder on the mountains.
The echo of the chorus broke the sidewalk—
People encumbered benches—vegetation—
No conspiracy controlled the census list
But it was misused

A husband and wife argue about Christmas and Chanukah,
They are formidable, the wild geese, even alone

Even far from China flying over east coast waves near here
At prodigal speeds alone and just above the water

2.

You say beyond I say in time beyond
And who knows whether the great painters of the old regime
Were not in fact political monsters?
Composing great annotations together for the wrong side?

It is the sieve of words the wild geese flying
The Luoyang exiles, the six vowels
And a thousand years later the Luoyang fire

The six avowals the six false promises the six days of creation the six sicknesses

Clogs approach dogs on the yeast white sand
By which we mean the murder of the seals

Doctors in nineteenth-century English novels
Approached their jobs according to their authors'
Views as to whether the culture might be healed
There were three quacks for every quail four quails
For every raven and one blind eagle.

But they reformed the blind craft and divided
Into pharmacists, no longer peddling their drugs
And the farsighted Oedipus the Cured

Some of the leaves were punctured while alive

3.

But here, in the diseased undercount
They thought the word marsupial was witty
Ti Yi failed to laugh at it on the haystack mountain and was banished
For not having a "sense of humor"
As they wrote with careful brushstrokes on the indictment

And there were boles and punctures in the paper
Left by the stylus of the people

And that was made a joke and the wild geese crying
Sounded like laughter or mourning to the official Listeners

Artful complaint is never as murky as it seems
All are freed by it—a little
And artful compliance never as unforgivable

Here is where shells insinuate clouds and mist
Into history
Despite the west wind
They work like scribes glad to be accused of too much
Obedience or obscurity. On the floors and walls they climb like chalk.
The parimutuel parodists flatter the roundcheeked
Laughers
Desperate to see themselves as merry
In the mirror they carry around with them.
They are sprung but not freed. They take dictation
From the cage of comedy.
It defines them.

Reformulation gathers the vowels in
As legal reform cannot

Summon us with chapters of return

4.

The cinnabar of banishment

The primed mountains are full of filial herbs.
Interns and residents traipse trellises or caves
Taking brief time off when they can to nap:
Each part of the body has its distinctive tiredness.
The heart tires in its own key of calling for sleep
In its own tinctures its own iodine; a feeling different from the weariness
Of the shoulders' gravel and the exhaustion of the differently graveled brain

Each bout of sleep denotes the rest
Of devotion, and is devoted to one of the seven parts.
It was all kabbalah, all the book of the body.

Now there are three hundred thirty-seven thousand
Days in the year, and a year is a dragon's empire,
And time writes down what the single leaves could not.
Promotion equals demotion the denotation of the soul

Refining cinnabar in a night furnace
Tinterns and interns glint in the inner kiln
They call the court the melting geodesic
Dome the igloo aglow the banished rabbi
Whose reticent political emotions guide the sefer

Hedging; the hedges
The cinnabar of banishment

5.

The bird and the leaf who resemble each other
In not staying lastingly on the tree
Are not friends, are unaware of each other.
They inhabit different corners of attention.

Their departures are at their own rates, statistically speaking.
They fold into their own collectives or unfold
Wingspans against the humors of each of their worlds.
They have no common reputations except in a language
Different from any here: they unfold in the fog.

from *Pataphysics*

Saints

◊   ◊   ◊

1) Knives of the Saints

I returned your book of poetry to the store.
I returned to the scene of the crime because once I'd had you
the words floated into a ribbon of type.
Because it was where we once slung violent hash.
I returned a favor.
I returned the box to its proper shelf
that made not sense to me smelling of lavender,
and it waited to be made into a miracle.
I came carrying my wings in my teeth.
I came to under the organza influence of your best slap.
I came out. I came around.
I came back like a cat, the kind from hell.
I came to believe I'd been returned.

2) Chives of the Saints

When the waiter said "you're *wel*come"
she was waylaid, completely soup.
Dumplings healed her. Broth sustained.
Between the server and the servee passed
an Olympic torch of familyhood, a fruit crepe
of happiness. She was thankful for being welcomed
into his arms like a brown rice bowl.
She was thankful to be so single, so unbetrothed
to the service she gratefully received.

You are welcome, she thought of herself,
an utter dish festooned with gratuity.

3) Lives of the Saints

Most are quite ordinary.
They speak in English, the tongue of regular paperbacks.
They read for awhile, looking occasionally away.
They get hungry at the usual times slated for hunger.
They do not write the menu in script on a chalkboard held by a ceramic pig
        in a toque.
They simply make humble but delicious
grilled cheese sandwiches, pressing their handprints
into the flaming bread, branding it,
blending ascientifically four kinds of cheese, including a dry jack.
They prefer to drink along a tomato juice.
They like to later drag a bicycle down from its stern hook and squeeze the
        wheels.
They like to spend time in the garage, damply almost dying on purpose.
Then they go back inside the split-level ranch and eat potato chips,
casually licking the bottom of the bag salt from their fingers.

from *The Canary*

Anyway

◇   ◇   ◇

Never than, the look
More than enough (wait a minute)
From the whatever, okay

A long way, the look
More than enough, okay
A long way, the rest okay

(Gasp!)—but still, as always, as ever
Close to the train, so to speak
And bang And bang bang, gossip basics

Zip on those legs, as always as ever
Close to the train, gossip basics
Zip on those legs, this is sunglasses

As in those movies, so who needs
In the olden days, keeps awake
One long grin, hard to say

As in those movies, a wonderful first kiss
One long grin, keeps awake
Without cuts, a wonderful first kiss

Molten days, because of lingering
Nothing's personal, including yours
Dawn on, fit for, plump be doing

Molten days, appear brief
Dawn on, fit for, including yours
Come hither forever, appear brief

Keeping on giving, everybody's great
And keep on, a few directions
The same language, forward to going

Translate from to, everybody's great
And keep on, forward to going
Translate from to, miss so much

There's money, same as money
Then there's money, the money
Then there's money, then there's money

There's money, there's money
Then there's money, the money
Same as money, there's money

from *SHINY*

Nostalgia of the Infinite

after Giorgio de Chirico, 1933

◊   ◊   ◊

Hands are touching.
You began in cement in small spaces.
You began the departure. Leaves restrain you. You attempted the departure.
A smile in sunshine, nostalgia.

I have lost my detachment, sparrow with silver teeth.
I have lost the doves of Milan, floating politely.

                    Recognize me, I shall be here, O Nietzsche.
                    We have skipped down three pairs of stairs,
they are not numbered, they are oddly assorted, velvet.

                    Recognize me in sunshine.
Bulletins permit us to be freer than in Rome.
Castles perched on a cliff.
Filled with pears and magic.

                    I am not detached,
bulletins permit us comb, fish of silver.
A part of the tower
(Year 1913) beckons to us.

from *No: a journal of the arts*

from *Baby*

◇　◇　◇

Baby. In Three Parts.

Baby has discovered a primal land of no name narcissism not because she
knows the meaning of narcissism and wants to convert self-adoration into
something invisible, filthy, eager, peppery with sweat, and universally
altruistic. Not because she even means to love herself. Intention switches
places with the disquisition of lungs bursting with her smarts withering
future word balloons. Next baby is in hiding. She is going to praise
something not worth knowing. No worth. No verdict. Salty lips wrangle
with mist. Clotted clouds devour a sky. The goodness of good words of
Kantian aesthetics blow amongst flimsy detail for the round world
amplifies a life of its own, a life on its own, an anti-aesthetic with revolt a
wish list or one and one and one steeped in spikes, fingers, and holes. She
the gargantuan fragment pulls on the thin lower branch of an oak tree
then pulverizes one and then another oak leaf. With these new forms of
flesh jammed into each of her fists she marches into Daddy's room,
mounts his seated lap, and smothers his forehead with the application of
leaves. Her father in this play begins his history of fretting for his little
girl, whom he predicts is destined for the life of the artist. Baby willfully
disregards the codes-tossed-in-fret, but as an afterthought, she presents
her father with an alternative: this is for nothing, for no one, for it and me.
Come here Daddy and look into the glands of a fearless flower.
"All thinking hears the indelible imprint of survival." Once upon a time
baby wallowed in trivia so that no one could associate her wallowing with
shame. Baby figured that if she could live in an inchoate world where
her actions were neither confirmed nor denied, some great force would
bubble up around her and we'd all turn into ferocious beasts. Her body
would dissolve into the Realm of Ferocity and she would live shamelessly
ever after.

The. Open. Box.

Baby in another era was running from room to room with her arm
thrust out and her finger bent in a peculiar position. She was making
a splattering buzzing sound. A black fly in the form of baby! That ran
splat, right into the television set perched on a little stool. A stool that
baby had used only yesterday. Wha's 'at? asked baby, pointing at the
TV screen. The tiger was there ready to whisper in her ear. It's a
dungeon full of dirt. Oh, zee, zee, said baby in wonderment pulling at
the knobs. Tiger realized too late baby liked dungeons full of dirt,
especially when description poured spontaneously out of tiger's
mouth. Baby loved the mouth of the tiger. Especially its sweaty lips.
So the TV, it was black and white, went pop, on. Baby sat down on
the floor with her entire hand in her mouth, her mouth sucking on
the hand, four and five fingers. In and out. While nutty adults in
miniature did all sorts of things talking in odd theatrical voices as
if they were talking to air and air could listen. The air has huge ears,
thought baby. She looked around all about her but could only feel
the air brushing lightly against her cheeks in that interstitial world
between now and then. In the meantime, the jackpot hobnobbing
of the nitwits and sad sacks on television had vanished. In front of her
was an emaciated child with huge ribs and a terrible listless look that
frowned on baby's chubby face. Baby fearlessly batted at the TV
screen. The baby's in the box. The baby's in the box! The baby's in
the box! The box! Open the box now!

Another Artifact.

Open lips for sucking and pouting were all stopped up with a plug
that wouldn't come out. Without result, lips and teeth tugged on the
plug of a wasp wasted object. Baby's hands were moist as usual so
she wiped them down the side of her shirt. But she couldn't pull
the stopper out even with the use of her wadded up shirt, which she
had finally struggled out of. A voice from behind her said, it isn't
supposed to open. Hands pried baby's digits away dislodging the
object, which was returned then to a shelf and set between a portrait
of baby and a kachina doll with green pants and something earnest
about it moving forward. For a minute baby looked around for her
shirt. It had apparently disappeared along with the door shutting.
Baby's lips moved in and out in a sucking pout as she contemplated
the wasp-waisted relic on the shelf. The object was obviously the
physical manifestation of the inside of a song bound up methodically
around the middle with twine. Such fortification caused baby to place
her hand two inches below her navel and rub there with a circular
motion. Her belly was getting hot and her body was tuning up. Eee
sounds rose clear and up into her throat from her navel. If there had
been silence, silence would have been pierced but the room was
always humming.

Next.

Small mean feats and regurgitation of memories made baby wild. She melted into the crowd and I frantically followed her certain all the while she would meet her doom before the fatal hour when moths let loose a scent that compels humanity to respire most willfully. Creatures fallen from grace including show horses and several unfortunate mud hens pranced and scuttled unwittingly through the compositional nightmare. Did baby know where she was going? Absurdity after absurdity stunted my search for baby. The moths swooped around a slanted tree. A derailed train lightly nudged its trunk, which was torn away slightly from its surface roots. Bankers and stockbrokers and sales people of all stripes marched up and down the sidewalks as invisibly as if they were in Midtown Manhattan. The sun was lowering slowly and I was frantic to find baby. If I were to call on a cop for assistance I would be asked for my credentials. These credentials, neatly tucked into my sock, were wilting with sweat. The stench would prove that I was a lazy and even abusive parent.

I thought I heard baby at a distance. When one loses baby, the body comes nearly undone. Your guts start to strangle your organs and your limbs take flight. Suddenly I recognized the location: San Francisco. This was good. I knew this town.

At nightfall, I thought I saw baby standing on a soapbox made of musical instrument cases stacked precariously one on top of the other. At an artificial height of four and one half feet she was a commanding young figure. Like gaudy acrobats, her dimpled arms flung up over her head every time she wanted the crowd surrounding her to cheer or egg her on. There she was, or so it seemed, exercising her rights to free speech again. As I approached, my view of baby was obliterated by onlookers. When I could see again, the musicians were unpacking the instruments from the cases: the soapbox had been dismantled. The musicians tuned their strings, sucked on mouthpieces, then began to play a sad song:

Hold me
Hold on
Waiting for curfew
To go home

It's night
Bright lights
Fling fear
Away

Hold on
It's night
Bright lights
Fling fear away

Let's play
A tune
Waiting for curfew
To go home

I left before it was over. And yet, it didn't seem to matter at all if
I stayed or went. Baby would be raped and murdered by now
kidnapped or placed in a holding cell at the police station or given to
a foster family or placed under observation in a social worker's clinic.
Or she would be hiding in the basement with some local cur and her
pups, feeding with the pups from the cur's nipples and drinking out
of the same water dishes. Someplace out there was the real, the reality
principle, even reality and realism all tied up in a bundle waiting for
the flood of investors to snatch the whole thing up. And that's where
baby could be found. But "I" I was left here in the imagination
strangling in the pearls before swine she'd smothered me with,
intoxicated by the false scent wafting around the urban rot of baby's
noisy dreams.

Again. The. Time.

Repetition and baby. Losing and tiger baby. Water in baby and curling.
Ears and accumulation. To know everything. Baby is entirely inside
baby. And then baby glides, a little boat, and not interruption. She
doesn't want an imposition. She seals tiger's mouth with her wet
tongue. This is tiger silent. A hand dances with a knee. Silently things
have fallen around baby. "The sun taking a bath," says baby.

Yelling. For. Fun.

Someone produces frequent groans. Flowers ornament the walls. Out
is getting out and being out. And being out getting out.

Mutations.

In the air cuddling with the wildest regions. Reproducing one
trauma after another. This is it. Life was getting longer. It was
becoming historical.

Mutations.

A face with red cavernous gashes and things possibly living in them.
Possibly pill bugs, dragon flies, freedom fighters, and tiny horses.
Then eyes as large and black as truck tires but with irises and pupils as
gentle and wary as a handsome mammal. Exaggeration is better than
bricks and squares. Baby's ancestors knew this and baby is holding the
hands of her ancestors. They all reject banality, drinking from the lake
with their necks curved in arches. Someday baby will declare that
people are horses locked in upright bodies. That most of western
architecture is a product of repression. This is why she cannot, will
not ever wear shoes.

The. Corner. Of.

The whole lot is now dark and out of sorts. The corner then finally
vanishes. Lashed. Lacerated. Then the pain is gone. Something too
hot to even sting exits the tongue along with everything.

Baby. N. Baseball. Song.

Baby was going to sing and then sing twice. The song was later attenuated when there was nothing left to ferry to the foreground of the forest, which had been the center of singing as baby experienced her lungs. Experience. Experience. She sang. She sang divided and then twice feeling the lungs of the forest as her own and then stepping back to observe herself as a phenomenon springing into readymade denomination from the head of an old god named Nietzsche. Or N. His name too had been clipped short like the song when she, growing tired and distracted, had less and less to ferry forth as offering, as person, to the forest, which was transforming into high speed blur. Tings like notes left distinct prints in non-voiced ground near voiced air. These were things baby could not experience or express. She recuperated her energies and opened her mouth. She thought she was going to taste tings. Then she thought again and thus was thinking twice. The singing was attenuated, clipped short. Minor distractions delineated something back in the brain that her lips associated with sucking. Baby's little body is a speedball. That's what someone remarked as she raced back and forth between the catcher's mound and the batter's plate. Someone was watching her play. She is her own ball. This someone was laughing so baby flew into sky and ground.

Note.

There they were. The notes clipped. Short, spread out. Deathless and. Without design. Baby was trying to decide if she should let go the cry pressing up through her chest when the sound of children distracted her. Were they surrounding her? The children are coming. The children are coming. She sang. Wailed. Rolled into a speedball and proceeded on her back and forth diagonal course from b. plate to c. mound. Baby was not a team player. The shifting universe had narrowed to one demand: do not give up the strip of inside field. Singing, wailing were trampled in the dust of a play that cut all others out.

Baby.
(For B and T)

Because this is the literature of ideas I cannot smoke a cigar. Baby had picked it up in the parking lot at the market.

Because this is the literature of ideas what just happened is a thought. Baby would give the cigar to Uncle Ted. Uncle Ted liked a musician named Sun Ra.

He was from outer space.

When baby's father inquired as to where the cigar had come from, the one that baby had wedged on the tight ledge between head and ear, baby had the answer. This cigar is from outer space. It was a surprise for Ted from Sun Ra.

Tragedy. Reconsidered.

You've gotta throw yourself at the other baby because you've been abandoned and forsaken. The other baby ridicules and ridicules. You are left left left there. Left and thrown down and the other baby gets under you and licks the wounds that gird the fine figure you cut when you are hiding the truth: you are just a baby. The other baby who has ridiculed and tormented you and who now soothes you with tongue and a special silence abandons you, goes to work, mercilessly. You baby of babies stand out, among the wild albatross, shining and shining "when the sun goes down."

Go. Down. Sun.

Be with baby under baby.

Knowledge.

Knowledge was being processed. It was in the argument machine and the driver of the machine was a god with the face of a man and the body of an inkbottle.

Knowledge.

White fuzz in the air froze on a screen. Baby danced the cancan which she'd seen imitations of on daytime television. Monarch butterflies hatched that day blanketing the scruffy shrubs with anxiety. Baby danced on the sidewalk. She choked a coke can with a jump rope. Then blew up a plane with her semiautomatic spitballs. The butterflies wanted nothing to do with her. When she trapped them with her little hands, they played dead, and when she opened her hands they wobbled on air pockets off into distant trees. These children, these children, screamed baby. What do they know?

from *Sal Mimeo*

Poe: An Assay (I)

◇   ◇   ◇

In "The Gold Bug," the overt finding of the treasure
is tossed out mid-tale like a bone to a waiting dog.
His stories were not intended for the canine heart that howls inside us,
though he fed it the tidbits it needed to stay near.

What could simply be seen, named, described was not his interest.
Half-close your eyes, he advised, to double the world.
The process of a discovery accomplished was his interest,
its after-savoring his appetite and his pleasure.

While he wrote, the peppered moths
of industrial London were growing darker with an internalized protective
      soot.

While he wrote, the last illegal slave ships were still coming in.

In his 150-year-old prose there is only one word you might recognize as
      archaic.

Omission his characteristic gesture;
stepping into the thought that thought cannot enter
his characteristic desire.

While he wrote, the ongoing, quiet famine of laborers paid below costs of
      housing and food.

While he wrote, the ongoing, unquiet emptying of the Plains.

These things happened under the culture's floorboards and behind its walls.
These things happened beneath the lids of half-closed eyes.

It is not precisely true that they are absent, though it is true they do not
      appear.

Whether they were for him
embraced or subsumed in his offered terrors cannot be known.

While he wrote, Turgenev, Goethe,
and this lithe-legged haiku of Issa from the other side of the world:

      Spider,
      do not worry.
      I keep house casually.

In Poe the worry is like the long-cooled lead in Baltimore house-glass, settled
      and clear.

from *The Threepenny Review* and *Poetry Daily*

For "Fiddle-De-Dee"

◇   ◇   ◇

"What's the French for fiddle-de-dee?" "Fiddle-de-dee's not
   English," Alice replied gravely.
"Whoever said it was," said the Red queen. . . .

What's the French for "fiddle-de-dee"?
But "fiddle-de-dee's not English" (we
Learn from Alice, and must agree).
The "Fiddle" we know, but what's from "Dee"?
Le chat assis in an English tree?

—Well, what's the French for "fiddle-de-dench"?
(That is to say, for "monkey wrench")
—*Once in the works, it produced a stench.*

What's the Greek for "fiddle-de-dex"?
(That is to say, for "Brekekekex")
—*The frog-prince turned out to be great at sex.*

What's the Erse for "fiddle-de-derse"?
(That is to say, for "violent curse"?)
—*Bad cess to you for your English verse!*

What's the Malay for "fiddle-de-day"?
(That is to say, for "That is to say . . .")
—*. . . [There are no true synonyms, anyway . . .]*

What's the Pali for "fiddle-de-dally"?
(That is to say, for "Silicon Valley")
—*Maya deceives you: the Nasdaq won't rally.*

What's the Norwegian for "fiddle-de-degian"?
(That is to say, for "His name is Legion")
—*This aquavit's known in every region.*

What's the Punjabi for "fiddle-de-dabi"?
(That is to say, for "crucifer lobby")
—*They asked for dall but were sent kohl-rabi.*

What's the Dutch for "fiddle-de-Dutch"?
(That is to say, for "overmuch")
—*Pea-soup and burghers and tulips and such.*

What's the Farsi for "fiddle-de-darsi"?
(That is to say for "devote yourself"—"darsi")
In Italian—the Irish would spell it "D'Arcy."

Well, what's the Italian for "fiddle-de-dallion"?
(That is to say, for "spotted stallion")
—*It makes him more randy to munch on a scallion.*

Having made so free with "fiddle-de-dee,"
What's to become now of "fiddle-de-dum"?
—*I think I know. But the word's still mum.*

from *Hotel Amerika*

Catholic

◇　◇　◇

1.

What can you do after Easter?
Every turn of the tire is a still point on the freeway.
If you stand in one, and notice what is all around you, it is a pile-up of
the permanent.
The churn of creation is a constant upward and downward action;
simultaneous, eternal. If you keep thinking there is only an ahead
and a behind, you are missing the side-to-side which gives evidence
to the lie that you are moving progressively.
If everything is moving at the same time, nothing is moving at all.
Time is more like a failed resurrection than a measure of passage.

2.

The drive from the I-5 along Melrose to Sycamore.
The drive up La Brea to Franklin and right then left up to Mulholland.
The drive along Santa Monica to the rise up to the right and Sunset.
The drive along Sunset east past the billboard of the man on a saddle.
The drive from the 405 up onto La Cienega and the view of hills.
The difference between nirvana and nihil.

3.

Thomas Aquinas was an itinerant thinker. His thinking rolled like a reel.
It went forward as a movement backward. His thoughts may have been
placed on the side like the eyes of many intelligent animals.

To mitigate pain he recommended weeping, condolence by friends, bathing, sleep, and contemplation of the truth.
He was the ninth of nine children and sent very early to a monastery. The Dominicans luckily had no rule about staying in one place. So he could walk from city to city, Italy.

4.

Legal thoughts were developed by the Dominicans when they were assigned the job of creating penitential acts that matched each sin. They had to study humanity closely and seriously. Thomas took on this task and it became his life-work, his Summa, his body of words that he called straw in the end. Something to burn.

5.

Human nature: what is it?

The source and the destiny of each life are the same: an unknown that is unknowable. Unknown before; around and unknown now; and unknown after unless already fully known before.

Every act and thought has to be measured against this that has no limits. Why?

Because the failure to grow and flourish and develop is a terror; to die prematurely without having found any consolation for disappointment is an injustice.
A person wants to be known, to add up, to be necessary.
The only way to assure that this can happen is for there to be a way to study each action in relation to its immediate objective and to its surrounding circumstance: who, what, where, by what ends, why, how, when. You can by these terms measure your action in the world, but its final objective remains the same: unknown.

6.

For some meditation, contemplation, prayer indicate that there is an emptiness already built into each body and it is that which (paradoxically) makes these persons feel at home in the cosmos.

7.

For others the hoarding of capital signals a loss of desire for any more knowing; it substitutes numbers for objects. It creates a safety net out of figures.

8.

The taste and smell of an action, any action, comes from its objective. This is the strange thing about relationship. What you desire is what creates your quality. You are not made by yourself, but by the thing that you want. It is that sense of a mutually seductive world that an itinerant life provides. Because you are always watching and entering, your interest in fixtures grows weary and your strongest tie is to the stuff off to the side traveling with you.

9.

Lemon-water light of California. Flattened with big boulevards and wandering men and women depleted at bus stops. Back alley bungalows. A terrycloth sash, evidence of neglect.

10.

The walk up Sycamore at night with Tom, looking in lighted windows and at varied architectures Mediterranean and Mexican. The warm night's pungent gas fume and flower.
Nights alone on Sycamore, grown children gone, windows open, bars and screens, my silver screen darting images onto my shirt.

The drive down La Brea at dawn to get onto the San Diego freeway with trucks and commuters catching the Stock Market opening in NYC. The lineaments of daybreak are silken tar and stars. Traffic is already on hard and Boston early morning news.

11.

Passions are eliminations, but they are critical to the body's survival, because they attract, command, and absorb; they make vigilant. Hope and fear, these are the two passions that loom behind all the others. I know a man driven by fear, and another one deluded by hope.

12.

Pain interferes with your ability to concentrate. A priest told me to prepare for the end while I am still mentally ordered. Old age can scatter the work of a life-time. Probably people should go *Sannyasa* as soon as they retire, and become wanderers, contemplatives, ones who act charitably all the day long.

13.

An ethics of intentionality must stay at a practical, measurable level, and never become abstract. Don't ever argue principles, my father told me. Stay with the facts.

14.

These scribbles? Stray ends? Ardor's droppings?

Illness has its own aura. And one who adores haloes can smell and see the aura of illness. A thick swimmer. Through the door, an odor. A mystifying stiff. Millions of them world-wide.
Geese are going over, raw as a jet stream, the windows open and a stick finger plunged into a science jar. Seedless.

Nature exists in a deep sleep, Eden's sleep. This is why watching and hearing the wind in the trees or the waves brings such peace. If Natural Light is the imprint of Divine Light, the word Divine is unnecessary.

15.

In some form or other, the deformity of the form is always potential as opposed to immanent. Perfection requires attention.

16.

Asshole or jerk? Which one gets to be President.

You know the man by the punishment he deserves and doesn't get. He can actually perfect his sin with malicious intent and no one will even notice.
Because we have an infinite disposition for wanting the good.

17.

The freeway passes the airport and its glut of traffic, the planes' bellies ballooning over the lines of cars. Bullets and bombs and parachutes ghost and worm their way out of them to cover the head. South lies ahead and more south, an opening to the sky bending down like the head of a lamb. I like the look of a mountain.
Mine eyes see the sun rising from mine east, they often have tears in them that will soon be blinding and blessing at the same time.
Long Beach and oil and electricity and the military built all the way to the beach—their forms the forms of insects who are empty of sleep.

Hills and fields around Irvine and the Lagunas. Field-workers bent over green and white. Now is the time for the Sixth International Brigade.
As I get older I don't remember what things are, only what they look like and are named. The way Los Angeles becomes hell at

night after being purgatorial all day.
When allegory enters time, it is the sign of profound danger.

18.

The Dominicans, a young order, were given the task of instructing
others in penances. Therefore, the study of human nature was
critical. They soon found out that studying human action was the
same as studying God and creation. Aquinas went on to discover
that all labor is study of the divine since the divine is everything
and anyone who lives is stuck inside the structure of God the
Cosmos. He was concerned with being, not doing. And his love for
the world was so intense, it infused his thought with compassion
for all things. He has been compared to Confucius, Sankara,
phenomenology. He makes it possible for some people now to
remain Catholic despite enormous misgivings and consciousness of
the Church's bad acts. He's not the only one who makes it possible,
but he is an important one because he is still considered an Angelic
Doctor of the Church, one whose thought remains foundational in
Catholicism. You can find his mind there, waiting, permitting,
guiding right into modern day life. He saw each person as an
important piece of a magnificent puzzle made by and for God.

Plummet into that mystery if you want to know more.

19.

Aquinas walked until he banged into a tree, and then he collapsed
and died soon after. He didn't want to write another line anyway.
Modest and bewildered until the end. He never stopped equating
joy with truth.

20.

I can't believe I can see. I can't believe I can hear. I can't believe I
can speak or think. What are commodities but evidence of lost

people. You cannot love a bathrobe so what can you love about
your own texture.

21.

The airplanes' bellies and bonnets loom over the freeway landing at
LAX. Ahead is south of south, Irvine, an opening to distance. I like
the look of a mountain of matter.

22.

The hills plunge down to the Pacific that I forgot to view. Six am en
route to work. Deepening as the sun warms and lifts. Rev and veer
and avoid exits at all costs. Rows of settlements will deteriorate,
designed to fall lightly flat in earthquake.

23.

Every turn of the tire stops at a halfway point to nothing,
Parmenides. To walk this walk would be better, to walk from
Sycamore Street to La Jolla.

One hundred miles.
The only end sought for in itself is the last end. It is always present
in us, after, after. The sky all around.
The completion of ourselves.
Everything we want is weirdly in everything we seek, so this is how
we know who we are, by what we want, by what we lack. The outer
tells the inner what it wants.

24.

Evil is the privation of good in any subject, it is a weakness and a
lack. This is why it is compatible with capital.
It may lack reason, or heart, or conscience, or empathy, it is a sign
of incompletion, it is an exaggeration of one quality at the expense

of others that must be banished in order for that one to thrive. Intention is hardly distinguishable from morality. It colors the action that comes from it with the shade of the desired end. The sad thing is that you can apprehend your goal as good and be wrong. Most of the time this is what happens and so you have the problem of judging yourself in terms of both intention and desired end, when things go wrong.

25.

Where did I go wrong? At the same place everyone else did?
Why did I end up living in unhappiness for so many years? Unhappiness was the desert, literally and figuratively.
Trees that don't move. Sun on dry dog turds. Black immobile shadows. Temporary infinity.
This was not home because my interior landscape was composed of wet, watery images—soggy brick, flowerpots, begonias, big morning glories, sloppy roads, and turbulent skies.
But something worse, generally, was occurring in the world around me, as it also occurred in me. The restlessness, the consciousness of a disappearing base and goal, the lack of home and civic engagement. I loved no city that I recognized.
Anything can happen under these conditions. Nuclear bombs, dirty bombs, small-time random murder, and abduction.

26.

At the marine training base, the second border of Mexico begins, call it San Diego County. The twin-breasted nuclear power plant beside the pap-white sea. America stops here.

America is not located in the small beads of sand, the pelicans, dolphins, or the arching erotic hills. Fish tacos and woman driving alone at dawn with immigrants packed inside the truck ahead of her. We have left America to the conceptual capitalists.
But so-called Americans have settled here, as on the West Bank of Israel where cheap housing for US Christians is expanding.

27.

A train runs parallel to its tracks and the freeway.
Eucalyptus border the road through Leucadia along the tracks,
heading south, the lettuce melting in the boxcars like a poor
film sequence.
The second border on the other side of the freeway crossing north
at the marine training base. Twin breasts of nuclear power plants,
the humping hills.
Women running alone at dawn, aliens sending money home, in
their wallets pictures of family and friends, love letters, addresses,
don't want to be here.
The canyons are groomed and pocked with bourgeois housing
developments that are built for eclipse. The spirit muscles its way
out of disappointment and follows the body laughing. Jesus after
Easter is laughing all the way down the road.

Tramps, boxcars, Marx, tacos, Dos Equis, rabbits uprooted and
fobbed onto parks, coyotes splitting into lonely wanderers, tractors,
tanks and brutalist walls. "This is the future," said a professor.
The ocean forms a raised screen at the end of every west-side road.
Strange how it lifts like that. Mustard carpeting the canyons.

28.

Night drive along Mission Blvd, left on Turquoise to get to the 5
south. Happy stop-offs, proximate ends, promised lands, ruthless
and armed RVs beside chugging little geezers. Old Town to exit on
Washington and up dazzled adobe trash to see the east out of a
plateglass window on Georgia, then back to Normal Street for chicken.

I am West or something. I don't know, but night clouds roll out of
the east as voluminous pitch that erases the stars.
I love being awake, someone said of her insomnia. She hid the
night in her closets and left the rest in color.
So nature remains but grace passes like a panopticon flowing its
light onto others in its slow circular motion.
Fugitive soul of the battered woman. She keeps running in search

of a safe-shaped geography. It could be as flat as the desert. You are obliged to follow your reason, even helter-skelter through the canyons. You are obliged because there is inside you a living soul that fears annihilation before happiness can discover it.

29.

If something you do is good for more people than you yourself, you can be pretty sure it is the right thing. (That is, it will make you happy.)
Speed, aptitude, certitude. Direct yourself towards action. It is imperative to find a virtue in itinerancy because this is the world now. People are either fugitives who want to go home, or seekers who don't want to go home. The movement of immigrants across borders brings much suicide with it. Imperiled people give birth to more children than people who are settled and comfortable.
The success of rabbits.
Sorrow weighs down your brain with water.

30.

All hope depends on possibility. Nothing much more. (But you can't have hope outside of an active sense of justice; and this complicates the processes.)

Both Buddha and Jesus preached contradictory messages depending on whom they were speaking to.

31.

The Egyptian women lied in order to protect the babies of the Hebrew women. God rewarded them for their lie. He gave them houses on earth. Moral ethicists are disturbed by this hypocrisy on God's part. But this is one way the notion of "person" is born. How is it lost?

32.

The intellect is contemplative.
Voluntary ignorance is a terrible social sin.
The embrace between faraway, freeway, and very near is air, breath,
oil, here.
Mouth and food. Going somewhere you don't want to be. How does
the will work. I don't want to go where I am going!
Peripatetic effusions.

33.

I pretend I trust surface truths, that I am moving forward, street by
street, and everything I pass, is passed. I have a goal, a plan, and I
receive what comes to me in the form of smell, sight, touch, sound.
The street that I can't see exists now in a state that will receive me as
I enter it and everyone else will enter the next moment at the same
moment as I do. The world is round and I am walking it. Time is
space.
I pretend that I can take a step, with D--th directing traffic and
earthquake and heartbeat and hate, is all I know of faith.

Doubt allows God to live.

34.

Sometimes you are privileged with a glimpse of the other world,
when the light shines up from the west as the sun sets and dazzles
something wet. The world is just water and light, a slide show
through which your spirit glides.

Reason is the dominant weapon of oppression. (Reason versus Person)
Reason without the other values becomes evil.
Reason where it lodges in me as an anonymous individual is
still oppressive but it works best in harmony with other passions—
people are depending on me is the main one.

But if I were president, I would reason the world into horrific war because I would not let myself feel compassion or hope. I would eliminate passions that contradicted my reason.

35.

Plato believed that criminals wanted punishment. In a sense they committed the crime in order to suffer for having thought up an evil in the first place. The crime was the proof of a worse evil: the mental plan. The crime allowed them to be punished for an intention.

In the same sense Aquinas knew that thought was contaminated, but he took circumstances into account and was not a judgmental kind of man, but he didn't have much truck with morose delectation, that kind of morbid indulgence in painful thoughts. Why, because they really undermine hope.

36.

I once spent a night in Dorchester, near Milton, near Massachusetts Bay, near Boston, Quincy graveyard and home. I don't know why I agreed to this, because it was something I didn't want to do. I felt sorry for the person who asked me, and no wonder. He was a tramp with severe medical problems. He had been given a couch to sleep on for one night and wanted me to sleep on a thin bed upstairs. He didn't care about me. Now I realize that I did it because I wanted to know where the ground of being weakens.

I think you can know more if you do things that are fearful or unpleasant, as long as they do not include hospitals or jails.

Wanting to know is what makes me do things I don't want to do. Wanting to know how far I can go with what I know.

37.

This is why I keep moving and only stop for the eucharist in a church where there are sick, vomiting, maimed, screaming, destroyed, violent, useless, happy, pious, fraudulent, hypocritical, lying, thieving, hating, drunk, rich, poverty-stricken people.

from *Chicago Review*

[Record]

◇　◇　◇

At St. Patrick's Day, and the Saint's death, plus 1,500 and 40 years, by the
　　　tradition
to hear the call of the deer, the thicket call, the creatures, the tide call, the call
at a Saturday, plus 1,500 and 40 hours, by the reckoning

Ed Dorn came to our motel room, talking to my mother and my brother and
　　　me and remarking on the rare chance it was to see all of us together
　　　at once
and then was gone and I after him with his keys he'd forgotten
and after my mother, on before me, and with hers too
and then everyone gone and not found
only a boy running down the street ahead of me, faster than I could ever
　　　manage
the good of aging

★

And when you die, or when you think you're dead, or when you dream
　　　you've died
your feet are turned backwards and your legs and loins but not your waist
and your arms embrace your head and backwards too and one of them waves
　　　goodbye to the air in the air
and the dancer on your belly whirls and reaches to regenerate the sun
and rides your body like a boat curved on into the sun
holding all you've ever done up like a ticket from amongst the snakes
and blossoms sway to tickle your navel, the entrance and the exit, the swivel
　　　and the plug, the cast and the release, and the call

★

Crows and redbirds   clear cawing and clear calling
and the quiet of Saturday, the quiet of Spring Break and the students gone
        and the students staying
and the cyclamen fading rosier and rosier from blood-crimson to the tide
        gone into and the turning

★

A small box on Ed's nose?   a little book?   (knows)   tickets?   the balanc-
        ing and the balance and the keys

★

"*You will feed others*"   "*I am the ghost*"   and the others are onions
and onions are worlds and worlds within worlds and water and corn
and corn is the hill spirit and the thicket
and long-leaved and long-eared and long-legged
and long gone and come again
and all long a-reach

★

And the cyclamen petals back blown back by the wind they nose into
sniff, hound snouts down, ears up, hard on the trace and long and hard
        a-hold

★

Hard, in the calling through

Hail, who is coming through

from *No: a journal of the arts*

from *Urban Renewal*

◇   ◇   ◇

XVI.

What of my fourth grade teacher at Reynolds Elementary,
who weary after failed attempts to set to memory
names strange and meaningless as grains of dirt around
the mouthless, mountain caves at Bahrain Karai—
Tarik, Shanequa, Imani, Aisha—nicknamed the entire class
after French painters whether boy or girl. Behold,
the beginning of sentient formless life. And so,
my best friend Darnell became Marcel, and Tee-tee
was Braque, and Stacy James was Fragonard,
and I, Eduard Charlemont. Time has come to look
at these signs from other points of view. Days passed
in inactivity before I corrected her, for Eduard was
Austrian and painted the black chief in a palace in 1878
to the question whether intelligence exists. All of Europe
swooned to Venus of Willendorf. Outside her tongue,
yet of it, in textbooks Herodotus declares the legend
of Sewosret of black Egypt, colonizer of Greece,
founder of Athens. What's in a name? Sagas rise and
fall in the orbs of jumpropes, Hannibal grasps a Roman
monkeybar on history's rung, and the mighty heroes at recess
lay dead in woe on the imagined battlefields of Halo.

from *Provincetown Arts* and *Poetry Daily*

King of Repetition

◇　◇　◇

I am none but king of repetition.
I am none but a soldier with naught but a mission.
    I am the hand with its finger always touching REPEAT—
    I am the winding street
    I am the windy street.
I am none but king of repetition.

I am none but king of supposition—
I suppose, then, I must take a position.
    I suppose I must await battle boldly,
      and shun selfish pleading; turn away coldly,
then sway the hot day into brazen submission.

I am none but king of repetition.

I am none but king of sad persuasion.
I am none but the salt for the sanguine abrasion.
    I am the finger of the hand that keeps the wound wet.
    I am the finger of the hand that you never forget.
I am the finger, the hand—this mad persuasion.

I am none but king of repetition.

I am none but king of opposition.
I am none but a soldier, pale malnutrition:
    I am the sickly stomach, and your lips and your eyes;
    I am your lips and your eyes
        and the things that arise.
I am none but king of repetition.

I am a liar with a folk song's heart.
I cannot start, and I cannot restart.
    I am the finger and the foot and the following eye
    which is present, which is prescient; a lie.
I am a liar, and the lying my art.

I am none but king of composition—
composing a song, a lie, a mission.
    I want to repeat
        and I want to repeat
    I am the winding street
        and the winding street.
I am none but king of composition.

from *Hanging Loose*

The Man

◊   ◊   ◊

Penis

Dancing away from your cars by the frond of the sea I live;
The ramparts are pure rectitude: cut parachutes and deep-sea powdered
      sugar,
A fine run in the silence of the rain—

Arm

        O blue cosmos
Run and financier! Why, there is a France of my up and at them tomb,
A lemon-ray of surreptitious canal sound
Which hops into a series of helpless land.

Mind

I am the mind, dazzling mind reader
Chorusgirl in frameups landslider
Definition by teacups heavier
Than your Pompeii.

Fingers

Shorthand the substitute ring me a rose panorama
Climbing western and shirt helpless
The beachless cat. Tomorrow containers!

Forehead

Ocean of Niebelungenlied! Romulus
Satie Mellon canard shoeflex Greene
Dairy farmer. Virus.

Nose

Oregon bell and carpet.
Leftover silverness. A bell. In a carpet.

Eye

He walks to containers. When the dancing tulip overflows.
The restaurant's a son today. It is sun today.
We throw its overwhelming into the free top that overflows
Blue, violet, purple, everything, the Caribbean ovaries.

Ovaries

What is it? Why am I here?

Wrist

A longer knee events will stop confines orange
Orchestra chocolate logy and snuffly contagious cough.
Reference.

Tibia

When the foreleg is blue
Covering the lanternslides with fluff country
Panoramic cuckoo raspberry weenie roast Canada seventieth
Catalogue white swans beer barrel publishing mouse ditch
Wristwatch.

Knee

With fennel pals the ranch.
The best nights in Arabia. Cotton punches. Rearward actions.
Possibilities will not grumble toward the cheated giraffe
Quietly bursting the cactus with tweezers of cherries,
Just as I cannot remember my norm.
Was bent like this? and is unlike this? Cardboards
Jinglebells and playing cards,
Showing bleachers in light gas.

Knuckles

The benches have always been auctioned.

Spine

The backache penny come niche a lesson
Boa constrictor easel pretzel nylon preaches ruffles
Dance elevators less and more dark
Sassafras receives me foghorn parenthood quietly duck
Penniless master and a nincompoop hallway
Which seasons come into and look.

Heart

Leopard spots. Why not be a dancer?
Trim summer. Is the hookworm conceived as a relative?
Bust the ocean. In Canada when they say "opera," she brings the nurse.
When silence intimidates the two opium eaters. Rats' legs for breakfast.
Tar and feather the oak tree's builder. Let your mind wander.
Over there. In all kinds of weather. Candy strips them. He builds a glider.
The bell-buoy is a captain. Hate the ocean's builder.
We scream to the sun for kindling wood. Suzanne ignites.
Listen when they say, "The peach is hollow,"
Because they're lying. Speak of the Renaissance. Describe the feeling beneath
    five layers of snow.

When you are in Romania, be facetious. And they will love you there.
Office furniture. Sailboat's blue mints. Calico shovels. Evening and Ireland.
See me handspringing my lookee breast of copper!
The larks bring me,
The dazzling earth has wended
Sunder. I ate lunch in the popularity engine.
She passed the benches. A dog-raffle just ended. Your song can't feel the motor.
        The referee has overalls.
Marching beside me I felt that breast of onion!
Looking into the trees. The afternoon was a sundial. Our wheels came too.
Suddenly my answer was changed: the shooting lemons ate whiskey a sheep
        gave a hornet publicity! an architect fell from his office!
Chloroform sat sweetly amused: O ranchhouses of green snow
Lectures, castles and rotations. Luminous yet fearless bevel,
What are we? You white bowlegged valleys! I am the happy rose
The working classes have arisen like bright
Seals, and burned the ships whose dark
Indications of blood swing cars by a mere nostalgic smell. Weaken, distinctions,
While passionate light
Darkens the formations. There is a pig on the fortifications.
Remember the star of Bethlehem? Cut dead the commander of the root.
Stand on this pier. Summer now brings its roomy cathexis.
By night the elephant is heard, and by day the water. Now it is day, she must
        depart. That way they hear nothing. It is a concert.
From far over the desert a crocodile begins. When they called on one another
        last Easter it was a rooster. Now a carpet begins to unfold for them.
She wants to be the first. He watches her like a cicada; and when he is no longer
        interested
The waters flee with them like sundials. The green cities sit down and laugh. To
        grieve in that climate!
He gives her a pair of angels. They vanish like originals. All is dark . . .
But last summer, I swear,
I heard a voice saying, "Blundering
Coma dancing wild ineptitude, seriousness cars delve orange white
And mother of pearl kimonos bleeds delight.
Investing aorta kimono suttee's quietness healthy pianos
Nought handles them for me like shoes."

Teeth

Coldly the knife is Montana

Torso

Run by the rink lace

Hips

Orchestra when foetal ice

Thigh

Carnival handball football millionaire
Yes I gave all my gold gives to
The chest, the shoulders, the armpits, the ears, and facial hair

Ear

We hand together

Facial Hair

Love and laughter

Armpit

The Earth Mother of silent things

Toe

Bastinado potato

Shoulder

Boiling

Palm of the Hand

Lobster scenario

Head Hair

And can't one gold give will not
Ecstasy domino shoe foot quiescent

Rear

Not to bannister forever and ever the bare

Skull

Rusting of hennaed springtime
Into an act the foot
Wills?

Thumbnail

Yet how can we be silent . . . ?

New York, 1953

from *SHINY*

To an Audience

◇ ◇ ◇

I knew the artifice would finally come to this:
      An earnestness embodied in a style
More suited to the podium than to the page,
      Half sight, half sound, an antipastoral
With which to while away a vagrant afternoon.
      The stage is set as for a play, with cotton
Clouds and cardboard trees beneath a foil moon
      That fails to illuminate the scene.
If you believed in me—if what I meant to say
      Resonated in your heart; if a tone
Held your breath and caught your feeling for the world;
      If my thoughts were thoughts that you alone had had—
The reality would be the same: the summer day
      Outside, indifferent to the other day
Tranquility and time conspired to create.
      This is my arena—this is the stage
On which I mean to live, an isolate domain
      Bounded by silence, inwardly consumed by
Music whose relentless cadences resume
      The speculations of that secret self
For whom to even try to talk to you is death.
      These are the stanzas of a single story,
Spun from unconnected moods that ebb and flow
      Across the surface of the day, from words
Implicit in my breath and spoken to a mirror.
      I get up, retrieve the newspaper
And read myself into a stupor. Then I write.
      I know these habits are a ruse, the tricks I
Use to keep the world at bay, to keep alive

The fiction of the soul as self-contained.
Yet even as I speak its character is shifting
        As the light shifts and I seem to hear
A disembodied murmur from the balcony
        In which I think I recognize my name.
What made me think that I could live apart from you?
        The folly of that thought now seems so clear,
With scenery and background drifting towards me as you
        Overrun this stage I said was mine.
My thoughts may try to hide themselves, to glow in private,
        Yet what animates the page is just the
Specter of a self existing in and through you
        As a forest finds itself in trees,
A city in its towers. This place is bathed in light,
        Revealing it for what it is, a crude
Pretence of thought, like children playing with some blocks,
        Unconscious and alive to one another.
Let my purpose hence be plenitude and patience
        In the hope that through their common grace
I might eventually attain that generous
        "Condition of complete simplicity"
That musing on the thought of you has let me see.
        I'm grateful to you then for all your questions
And objections—for indeed you *are* objections—
        And that is all, for now, I have to say.
Let us conclude though with some resolutions: to
        Abjure these fierce conundrums of the soul;
To quit this theater of dreams; to walk as one
        Into the light of ordinary day.

from *TriQuarterly*

Ignis Fatuus

◇   ◇   ◇

Something or someone. A feeling
among a swish of reeds. A swampy
glow haloes the Spanish moss,
& there's a swaying at the edge
like a child's memory of abuse
growing flesh, living on what
a screech owl recalls. Nothing
but a presence that fills up
the mind, a replenished body
singing its way into doubletalk.
In the city, *Will o' the Wisp*
floats out of Miles' trumpet,
leaning ghosts against nighttime's
backdrop of neon. A foolish fire
can also start this way: before
you slide the key into the lock
& half-turn the knob, you know
someone has snuck into your life.
A high window, a corner of sky
spies on upturned drawers of underwear
& unanswered letters, on a tin box
of luminous buttons & subway tokens,
on books, magazines, & clothes
flung to the studio's floor,
his sweat lingering in the air.
Years ago, you followed someone
here, in love with breath

kissing the nape of your neck,
back when it was easy to be
at least two places at once.

from *The New Republic*

The Dark Continent

◇ ◇ ◇

Intimacy if we can [intimate] an
Other way what difference our hands
Unrest conceive division

what difference/s our hands conceive
thighs. tightness. tense. trill. trail or trial?
"Let's be logical."

"Let's be logical."
Your panties. I was
slipping off.

Yes.
Let us be
logical.

To get to. Between legs.
To get to. Between lisps.
It is a dark passage we share in the lightout to get to lips.

"We have to be logical." You orgasm
"I'm on my period," you say.
I taste but cannot confirm.

I take of my pants.   logic
I take of my shirt.   logic
I take of my socks.   logic

logic
logic
logic

There are halfway houses found only on the elliptical
orbits of mad poets. There are halfway houses in need of
us. Need. Yes. There are mad poets needing.

Show me the intersection that finds
us unlocked to the barrenness of words
on this continent. we cannot refuse this night

"What do you want to do?" you defer to me. Hours
later in the curtainfilter of your bedroom sunlight you say
"that would make a great picture": my hand rest

your crotch. What Culvert. or Palisade. Rampart. or Strife.
Subduction. or Sanctuary. We may speak littorally and we may
never speak literarily of unknown reconnoiter. my fingers

probing, my other hand resting a Corona purchased from
the night before at the 7–11 on Taraval, we watch the bottle sweat
to my wrist and to "the hinge" of your body and

to your three week old queen futon delivered the same day I drove
you home for the first time from class. Is this Arcadia? and I/you
convert to communion and/or conjunction fjording

intersections of canal or street
intersections of incandescence
intersections of influence

"Milk for the laity" asked the common
priest to his uncommon flock court holding
hot milking cold cow cowl warm

At what altar we acolytes were discomfited
To what premise we were unfrocked
At what first intersection we deceived fear

from them
to go
to meet discalced and armored

of our awkward apostasy we proof images
track deviant lines
disobey evenness gravity

with nimbus cropped and/or uncropped
you/I Arcadia. A stop on what lost week
end of roads

your missionary position what is
your unmissionary position what is
what confession is your duress

the pediment firms us on the shoulder of interstates
the fixating highwaymen's stroboscope
the drunken tumbleweeds

have you ever jerked to the side
have you ever measured the fallow shoulder
have you ever dissolved into the rearview mirror

for shadow
for devil
for flower

meeting sins
meeting revenants
meeting innkeepers and strays

confident in abandon and antiphon
confident in eccentricity
confident of gravity's elastic

and is your dire need your dyer need your diarist need
helmet and sprung for the charged gun's inkflow
what rupture what structure strop and strap

to restrict
to cohabit
to unknow and undo

pages to
directories to
codices to

novel
flash
suddenly

what boxstrut what boxtrap
scissors and caesuras is
palimpsest at what angle I want to ask are

you conceiving deference
our hands believe impersonate
and your navel I stare

Have you ever been in
a woman's vagina for seven hours
ask them I will

It was fluid
It was wet
It was flowing

It was fluid wetness flowing warm hours
Like a hot tub outdoors and the stars
lifted on chlorinated thermals

It was fluid wetness flowing seven warm hours
Like a hot mineral spring and the stars undone
by rhizomous thermals

It was fluid wetness years flowing
into seven seconds
Like a womb before it becomes heretical

or I might say Bison Brewery's Hibiscus Hard Ice Tea
I drank too much
or I might say *I freaked out on acid*

or I might say the Chiropractor passed the pipe packed of Train
Wreck after a moribund game of chess
or I might say Park Street's Arco's 87 sold at $1.35 a gallon

Ever drive to Lompoc for Pea Soup
Take the Grapevine to hear poets read in Santa Monica
Ever lighten the trunk of the spare transmission and remove

volumes of poetry from the back seat of a Tempo and replace them
with Snickers, shrimp Cup-O-Noodles, and Red Bulls,
caffeine and ginseng pills and take the southern route to

Providence
Ever look forward to the next rest stop or gas station hoping
for directions to Arcadia?

Dark passages wait for us
Tollkeepers wait for us
Billboards wait for us

"That would make a great picture" you say again
sleeping my head off
on the down of your pubic hair

I stare at calamity avoided
I stare for finity
I stare between drinking—at what

fright filled hour do I stop sleeping
this waist land a rest stop
And I ask you is it safe

that I am an intellectual. a yes and a no question
And before I subsume my tongue into your navel I say
omphalos and you understand the center of the universe

we both read mythologists and psychoanalysts
they did not teach me Greek but a lover of Bartók
who said 7 years ago my smoking was my girlfriend

substitute. You now wish to smoke
and are not our bodies smoke
you/I arrhythmic phantoms in Arcadia?

Don't you see at what focal stop?
Don't you see at what colored corrected lens?
see what degenerate vision our fetal positions

trembling hand caving calyx
lynx what slink wolfishness
what dropsy what drink

at what borderland barstool
at what busdepot lockerroom
at what famished evening writers' event

what impenetrate your inselberg
no novice berm rises rises
rotund or infirm

no covenant or hackneyed convent
cistern or sewage
trowel or towel or tower or towering

who lurks in what colonial acropolis waiting to steal
aboard streaming convoy from steaming convoy
cruising edge of empires

what journeys to seizured spice islands
of epileptic serpents and serpent-eating eagles
of fledgling mango princes and roseate princesses?

A blessing.
Safety.
Salvage.

insolitude.
unvanishing.
conceiving.

Yes.
They are mad
poets need unrest.

Yes.
They are mad
poets need undress.

Privations and depravations and impregnations
and are they shades and/or striations
you ask when we emerge what will we say to them

Arcadia
Arcadia
Arcadia
Arcadia

from *Rapidfeed*

After Mahler

◊   ◊   ◊

A thousand minutes came out of the tottering state.
The bed of thyme moved within its bearings like a dream.
He answered, "tomorrow."
Someone else was screaming on the radio; people laughed.
The cat has been dead for some time now.
The wedding party's bright joy looked strange from the streaking jet.

Meanwhile persons are moving around outside. They have decided to foreclose on
options pertaining to the new world. Instead, to allow themselves to live in a world
neither new nor old, but which abides as in a balloon floating untethered
above trophies and noise so that

                    truncated, wren-shrunk

    Pentecostal shade
              harp rubbed under Mahler's tent (his abundant farewell
                   to Alma's rage)
      after all   the part that was said and the part that was done
            the conductor in his care   so one was forced to go
                 back
          to how it might have begun after all
              the century that leaks its tunes into the summer air
                refuses to call

                  to call is to ask   break a silence   but the music
after all it is music   song-spiraled
      and the landscape detained   across a field   into a night   in which we
learn only the pornography of sight
      its ocular target

              see see see

from above the tents and the persons milling about
in their robes

                they are the disciples! silence them!

           And if they are merely birds   flocks rising in circle
like smoke without song   *see see*
      we cannot hear the tremulous strings   nor the soprano   glittering
            in the heat of the tent
          the conductor mouthing her words   not that.

Sun, making its way east and east and west of the river
where the ivy is not poison and the trees not weeds. And this or that spins i
the final cycle, its systemic will. Do not butter the toast, do not come
like a ghost without shame, a promise adumbrated
against the cry of any nocturnal creature.
All against one, and the philosophical questions
on a far continent like so many markets.

Nor that either.

Conditions above the smashed agora with the cowboy riding sunset on his
mechanical cart, his small mouth and child's
incontinent whine. Casinos in full play, paying for
assault, moving to the rush of coin. And still we did not speak, did
not know to whom to speak, muttered at lunch, gave each other
proofs of care, one to
one, but did not come to the table to hear our fathers, they were dead, our
mothers, they were busy, our neighbors, they were elsewhere, our lovers, th
were not listening. Listen. This is a lullaby. Listen.

               from *No: a journal of the arts*

Sound and Cerement

—"mu" thirty-eighth part—

◊　◊　◊

Caught in coastal weather, came
    in from the rain, they the two,
we who will have been none . . .
    It wasn't an epic we sang had
    there been a song we sang, heroic
                                waste
    around us though there was. The
    beloved's long-distance voice
was what it was. Muse meant lost
    in thought it reminded us, erstwhile
    epiphany, snuffed . . . It was all
                        a wrong
    turn or we took a wrong turn. All the
    roads ran off to the side and we as
well, we of the interminable skid . . . We
    were they of the imagined exit,
                            he
and she of the adaptable tongue,
    teeth, lips, mind's own sacred
    ass-cleft and crotch, we of the
                            exiguous
fit . . . Erogenous mind's dilated aperture . . .
    Cloth tore, ground gave way . . .
    World being anything but, we
    retreated, each the other's remnant
                                wisp,
    remnant caress kept only in sleep . . .

Fleet release the embrace made myth
of, arms' tight winding and wrap a
kind of cloth, cerement the skin itself.
   A spun sound answered us inside
                              and
   out, revenant, runaway love the least
of it, run though we did even so . . . The
   lost one's attenuated kiss was what
                              it
   was, the beloved's long-distance
                              breach
   and bedevilment, beckoning we broke
loose from. There was fold on fold of
   cloth and it was us, caress claiming
      myth a burial of sorts, cerement the
   spin we rode rode us, raveling arrest
                              un-
done . . . A republic of none the one included
                                    us,
      no word to speak it with, dumbstruck . . .

      Beginning to be the end it seemed . . .
   Ending begun to be come to again. Ending
going on and on . . . Wanting the world,
      what of it was ours not enough. The
                              sun
   rose, night notwithstanding. Came up,
hung deep in the wet sky. A kora's
   tight strings assisted it, launched it,
   held it for us to see. The sun was one of
   us it said. What it meant by us lay
                              cloaked
   in peal, ping, fado, world wanted only
for the sound it shook loose, Portuguese
                              tremor,
   trill . . . What wasn't us we had no way of
   knowing. What it meant by us was
   unclear, us included so much, sun
      seemed an alternate cloth . . . Beside

ourselves all night, no sleep. We
                            were
they whose bed was anything but. They
                                  lay
  awake in our sleep, we in theirs they
intimated, a song of song's end had there
  been one, a broken song we'd have sung
                               had

    there been
    a song

•

Reminiscing the wet of each other's
   mouth, recollected their boned
   embrace. In a hot room haunted by
    snow, the intractable two
                        in
   disarray . . . Borne away by who
   knows what. Were it a bus, relegated
to the back of the bus . . . A politics
articulate of late of late let go, a
    pool of remorse we fell into,
                       it
   might've been us in back . . .

                       We who
   rode in front rode as well in disarray.
Time's raw inroad it was, it wasn't
   a bus . . . Heaven it was we were in,
   not knowing we were. Hell was not
                     knowing.
We were in hell . . . So it was in the
kingdom of Nub. No way could we
   see past our noses. Dust got in
                   our
   throats, noses, eyes, fell all around
                us . . .
   Dust was rub's accretion, Nub's
                   inces-
 sant regress

•

Stark light the day I saw thru. I
too spoke with a shell on my
     voice, tongue a thick worm in
my throat. I was at the beginning
                              again,
     wanting to undo and redo what was
done. I was only what was left . . .
     Nub was being what was left, I
was Nub. Nub was being remnant,
     regret. I was debris, I was what
                              was
     left. I wore a mask made half my
                              face
     numb. One side hairless, the other
     unshaven, talked, ate, drank
                              with
one side of its mouth, numb side
     confounding what the quick side
felt. I was only what was left . . .
                              I wore
     a mask made half my face grow
     stubble, stubble side scrambling
     what the slick side felt. I was only
                              what
was left . . . Of late looked at from another
                              side,
     all sides . . . Out, over, either, both, I
                              was
     what was
left

It was getting to be the end again,
day done up in black, night white,
   edge along which we fell, thought,
falling, this is what the songs all

                           meant . . .
   All the songs were ecstatic,

                     lovestruck.
   Hearts bled . . . Violins . . . A worm was in
      my brow, bit me, heart's own target,
toyed with, I was only what was left . . .

      Abbey Lincoln sang a Sufi lament.
      Truth blurred if not blue, blue, bereft,
   face never seen they say . . . Lookless,
      faceless, voice heard in hell, life love

                              alluded

         to lifted, love's
         laryngitic
address

         from *Hotel Amerika*

HARRY MATHEWS

Lateral Disregard

after an observation by Kenneth Koch

◊　◊　◊

Shall I compare thee to a summer's bay
an orange cliff rising from its waters to the east
to the west a slope of reddish earth whorled with gray olives
between them an arc of rock, then sand, then little port
four houses of blue-washed rubble and red-tile roofs
and below them under broad-leaved vines a terrace with tables and benches
from which at noon the smoke of golden bream grilling
brings a gust of longing to the wayfarer as he looks over the bay
from a bluff down which a dusty zigzag path
leads to a straggly cluster of fig trees near the water's edge
(their first fruits now ripened in July sun)
to whose left on flat rocks ample nets have been drying
to whose right on the sand—green, yellow, green, red—four fishing craft
rest through the languid hours of the blue day
only at night taking to the clear dark waters
through which their bow-lights beckon curious fish
for nets to scoop from their nimble careers
to be shaken over the decks in slithering heaps
and at dawn the boats coast home between brighter blues
the glory of the world suffuses earth stone and leaf
land and sea reaffirm their distinction
in an exchange so gentle that the wayfarer briefly believes
he has been suspended lastingly in newborn light
the happiness and rightness of the morning
no longer dreaming plowing on through thick mud?

from *SHINY* and *Jacket*

STEVE McCAFFERY

Some Versions of Pastoral

◊   ◊   ◊

PREFACE

Et in Arcadia ergo points to everywhere. Semantic stability laid
smooth across cyclic ridden-epoch pages of remainders. It is the
theorized ambrosia and all that's deaf against light among the swamps
of somewhere. Chapter gathers grey did I live in it? Fleece of the
place changing name to four-footed high-forehead country chin.
The Pleistocene in discourse law of moulds surprised by the dash
half-past Pan ideology ellipsoid fragments seen in the water as Cuddy,
Mopsa, Blowzibelle ex-sensual course to evolution through etching
sideways into text material avalanche idyllic thought through bogs
and dewlap steering a race to the tunnel shore. Went into walking
wearing eyes on the heart because splash accumulation hints history
against the helmets. Thistle oval apertures a tree food glossed onto
morning. *Un détachment de la troupe sous le conduit de Monsieur Logique
c'est arrivé.* In such manner cart-paths hand Truth a palimpsest of
levelled bridges versions of pastoral and the lightest possible stake in
this: is speech.
Comes round on the road

from reading

etching spheres as continents

then strolls with a flute into dialect

and signs it.

1
for Robert Stacey

When I awoke I saw sheep
eating people, small children
actually, on an iron ground,
executive summers populating landfills
with a quote beauty unquote
turned to dust when written about.

That's it.   For stanza one.
The man takes a walk from dictionary to landscape
turns away in Old French
                nothing happens.   Afraid of death
Arcadia's withheld
'til stanza three.

2

Cloister my lady
the mind's back
-yard,
but
psychologically
a parlour space
with its pet dog additive to sky
line-top lit   room-tomb
modern junque tub at the age
of seventy-five
Dulce est desipere in loco   coming via
Horace as
the pleasantry of non-sense
in
due place

3

Sunny black-eyed Susan
with orange tongue
and disappearing rail tracks
for your eyes
what a surprise melts
the disproportionate esteem
of dream-team cupboard laundry
thinks
a shirt needs dirt
to really matter
knows
the temperature a kidney melts at
shuts the book
plumps turkey cook-mark
snows
to make the park become
a photograph by Manet
signed by Blake

5

The bridge is a heaviness across itself
the bridge must cross
so not to choke   the river.

Eventually, Mom became late with supper,
and Dad
made HIS appearance between Eleanor's dictatorship
and Robert's microsoft democracy.

The front lawn is where all the language stands
in Bermuda shorts.

But the sprinkler system   still remains unthought.

6

Sweet milk
white
snow
thy winter's in a pail

I have a night
once called the tongue
for rhymed quatrains
the station vacant from
the stain.

and plantains too!
sweetened by
a legacy of transit-trust
must in the rigid wind
stained, changed tympani
regency of stars

banana baas.

7

Go figure it

the bearded man in a cup
ending it

not until

now

in a shroud-snow
the sheep

occurring
in

the shepherds

8

Perhaps Paul Celan is the crematorium built especially
for Language Poets.   Perhaps
no things but in ideas.   Synaesthesia, the history
of rhyme, the geography of rhythm: a snowdrop
offered to a sixth sense
and having signified Mount Monad
changes
to a pledge, a promise not to dis-locate the hooves
of that animal whose origin names speed the pathos
ad infinitum   in the Muse's neck
exalienated now inwardizing
across the negativity exposed by the slipper
on the footnote
under the difference between
an elasticity and a language.

A thing is a place
in the touch of the world.
But all the hands are long gone here,
in the orange sector
and should it not be posited
it should not appear
in itself, as a face, a city's eyes, the pectoral
episodes before being, the curl
in a kind of chance yet not
random in its own
interpretation of the execution.

"Imagine someone pointing to a spot in the iris in a face
by Rembrandt and saying 'The walls in my room should be
painted this color.' "

Eye into art
even sense into language
the technique of the details suddenly
a stop-gap calculation half-zoned between
the finite and somebody else, not visible
yet scalar and in geometry

a force flooding
all the transits to the promise of a different world
than place
something less visual and yet vital
in arranging a sonorous life as speech and power
its friendly fate concrete
as God is
damaged and sanctified
in the metonymy named Auschwitz

almost a place to call cosmos
in the short quartet of which
there never can be
                    a discussion.

AFTERWORD

An hour through this clock is an absolute urban urge for
a sitting rung
voice to metaphor meat becoming scarves at a bullfight
later belief as power still lodged in familiar groups
pretending night falls a quadruped authority
artillery follows years to pools where sheep as relay in relaxing
stipend for genre
the luxury if arms where guns blow off comparison
divisible as unique find when sounds miss traffic
night drizzles out event by spot of big spit thing

agronomized escritoire.

The second landscape:
cabbage blisters in a final ambiguity
community diggers ingesting disappearance
a doctor's note in faded Latin as the all-extending fossil calls up
object moment brick fails thinking penetrates the same unknown

would you agree?

Led by consideration of a necessary principle of retroactivity?
A scheme-bend altering the dominant?
Or is project simulacrum still the Eastern Star?
Sky coils completed actions writing words?
Mathematics in a folded cloth fed silence into chair?

No.   Anatomy is Fauvist.
Seeds enervate then think.

Transposed umbrella to the negative space known as rip shore
sleet Asia calling
sulphur tendency to piss in exact streaks of virtue
neurosis in a bottle rack   atelier composure to the opposite directive
that I have sensed whenever the pizza comes a white wireless warms the stove.

The Voice coughed then put itself in brackets

(Ate in Acadia Eggo?)

Mentality's the flat I've never moved from[.]

from *TriQuarterly*

K. SILEM MOHAMMAD

Mars Needs Terrorists

◇   ◇   ◇

1.

:.:.:.:.: alien parasites
:.:.:.:.: alien slave ship survivors,
:.:.:.:.: alien teenagers in 1950s Florida, sex
:.:.:.:.: terror and destruction, terror
:.:.:.:.: designed to part dumbass teenagers
:.:.:.:.: some now very wet
:.:.:.:.: romantic, the republican
:.:.:.:.: told me of their terror
:.:.:.:.: outfit for ?I?ma slave
:.:.:.:.: a fundraiser for republican
:.:.:.:.: and wet buns contest
:.:.:.:.: parents talking about sex
:.:.:.:.: of here 7.battle him republican 8
:.:.:.:.: 8.we are 138 9.teenagers

2.

:.:.:.:.: 1.tn t. (terror
:.:.:.:.: grind 1.monkey business 2.slave
:.:.:.:.: 1.dead & bloated 2.sex
:.:.:.:.: pie 9.plush 10.wet
:.:.:.:.: mind-controlled slave
:.:.:.:.: affirmative vote regarding the wet
:.:.:.:.: to malign fathers and teenagers
:.:.:.:.: and engage in sex
:.:.:.:.: world, now we need teenagers

:.:.:.:.: few goofballs hauling their wet
:.:.:.:.: breasts plump and round such that
:.:.:.:.: needs more focus on sex
:.:.:.:.: a nation of former slave
:.:.:.:.: are two types of terror

3.

:.:.:.:.: comes with wage slave world
:.:.:.:.: technofa cism theory, Red Terror
:.:.:.:.: "many amongst the fair sex
:.:.:.:.: "pretty red roses, wet
:.:.:.:.: "reigning terror I'm just
:.:.:.:.: burnt out corporate slave
:.:.:.:.: sex dwarf
:.:.:.:.: as if it was all a gory, wet
:.:.:.:.: terror odyssey the exile list of terror
:.:.:.:.: in kidnapping and enslaving women as "sex slave"
:.:.:.:.: the terror is acknowledged that they have
:.:.:.:.: power within the republican
:.:.:.:.: porn movie) gotta their teenagers
:.:.:.:.: "Teenagers from Mars

4.

:.:.:.:.: in America the teenagers
:.:.:.:.: units touch spoke sex
:.:.:.:.: slavery slaver slave Slav
:.:.:.:.: dispensing with his "white slave"
:.:.:.:.: out of raw terror
:.:.:.:.: was big and black and stank like wet
:.:.:.:.: wets wetness wetly wet
:.:.:.:.: terroristic terrorist terrorism terror
:.:.:.:.: teeth teens teenagers
:.:.:.:.: republics republicans republican
:.:.:.:.: 133, 114 old, 660, 112 sex, 84
:.:.:.:.: 121, 11 ant, 6, 11 slave

:.:.:.:.: 10, 3 tiring, 0, 3 terror
:.:.:.:.: 0, 2 mound, 0, 2 teenagers

5.

:.:.:.:.: sexes sexed sex
:.:.:.:.: go out and have sex
:.:.:.:.: tie shirt suit wet
:.:.:.:.: male person has sex
:.:.:.:.: it a crime for teenagers
:.:.:.:.: has always picked up on the sex
:.:.:.:.: thanks to my former slave
:.:.:.:.: 3978 comfortable 3977 wet
:.:.:.:.: jay 937 divorced 937 teenagers
:.:.:.:.: 904 strips 903 slave
:.:.:.:.: teenagers think that
:.:.:.:.: dirty bombs will hit the USA at anytime
:.:.:.:.: in America—bin Laden because he spread terror
:.:.:.:.: was 140 pounds, soaking wet

6.

:.:.:.:.: welcome to Iraq Chat Opinions
:.:.:.:.: just fuckin' up your sex life,
:.:.:.:.: curled back in terror
:.:.:.:.: 1813 marvelous 1813 republican
:.:.:.:.: 1513 achievements 1513 terror
:.:.:.:.: United States, that teenagers
:.:.:.:.: image of the republican
:.:.:.:.: having lots of sex
:.:.:.:.: the of and to a in that is was he for it
:.:.:.:.: with as his on be at by
:.:.:.:.: spite soil runs republican
:.:.:.:.: attend absence windows wet
:.:.:.:.: stained spots slipped slave
:.:.:.:.: "my wife, panties wet
:.:.:.:.: "like some colonial slave

7.

:.:.:.:.: chest trembling treat threatening terror
:.:.:.:.: to death the nine teenagers
:.:.:.:.: republican leader urges new
:.:.:.:.: right to better sex
:.:.:.:.: *wet 'n' svelte:* Jennifer
:.:.:.:.: panties wet with excitement would gasp
:.:.:.:.: Osama bin Laden's terror
:.:.:.:.: to end up in the attic (engaged in a private sex
:.:.:.:.: this time of year going: ?damn, my feet are wet
:.:.:.:.: 7829 trees 7809 sex
:.:.:.:.: 1363 discount 1363 terror
:.:.:.:.: balcony 898 nuisance 898 teenagers
:.:.:.:.: involved in the black slave
:.:.:.:.: and sticky cold and wet

8.

:.:.:.:.: the republican party has degenerated
:.:.:.:.: in the face of terror
:.:.:.:.: probably calls up phone sex
:.:.:.:.: while they were teenagers
:.:.:.:.: work for NOTHING) as slave
:.:.:.:.: the massacre of teenagers
:.:.:.:.: fucker smells like wet
:.:.:.:.: "I am a republican
:.:.:.:.: "your ancestors had sex
:.:.:.:.: sliding around her fat wet
:.:.:.:.: pussy—formalities of wet
:.:.:.:.: she might Hoover up teenagers
:.:.:.:.: the sex was so good that
:.:.:.:.: uninitiated multitudes to the terror

9.

:.:.:.:.: sex beasts TWO sex
:.:.:.:.: regime him group sex
:.:.:.:.: he so often wet
:.:.:.:.: Tower Records tower terror
:.:.:.:.: terrible terrible terror
:.:.:.:.: reproductive reptials Republic
:.:.:.:.: of Texas Republica republican
:.:.:.:.: Teri Hatcher sex
:.:.:.:.: teen sex videos navel wet
:.:.:.:.: tie shirt suit wet
:.:.:.:.: tie shirt suit wet
:.:.:.:.: he is a republican and
:.:.:.:.: more than 140 pounds wet
:.:.:.:.: ANIMALS Japanese Irish republican

10.

:.:.:.:.: rabbit valley slave labor
:.:.:.:.: and sweet pictures of teenagers
:.:.:.:.: frozen in terror
:.:.:.:.: parents and hitchhiking teenagers
:.:.:.:.: terror: a female Klingon
:.:.:.:.: indentured servant: a slave
:.:.:.:.: who BEAR infants, BORE teenagers
:.:.:.:.: dares not is a slave
:.:.:.:.: fine art of getting wet
:.:.:.:.: a programmer's approach to sex
:.:.:.:.: what comes after sex
:.:.:.:.: cars and vote republican
:.:.:.:.: we are born naked, wet
:.:.:.:.: full of surprises and terror

from *Kiosk*

8 Little Theatres
of the Cornices

◇ ◇ ◇

1) Theatre of the Stone Chapel (Abades)

In one of its cornices are the two boots of a man
In one of the stone canzorros
If you listen you can hear him walk
His walk is stone and
his gasoline is stone
and his quill is stone

that's why he hasn't written
because his quill is stone

that's why he hasn't come yet
his gasoline is stone

that's why at night you hear him walking
his boots are stone

even his field of corn is stone
and his mother is water

2) Theatre of the Hope of a Cebola (Santiso)

In the hills there is no hay
but rain

no hay for a hayrick but
small rivulets singing the grass down

an onion has fallen off a high cart
the chest of the high cart has gone past the hill

if pressed with a shoe an onion toppled
may take root

will a shoe ever find it
how can we know

will the onion find a mouth to eat it
how can we ever know

In the channels of water:
small blue rivulets of blue

3) Theatre of the Millo Seco (Botos)

I am in the little field of my mother
her field touches
oaks of the valley
and I touch the faces of my corn

opening corn's faces
so that my hands touch its braille letters
The face of corn is all in braille
the corn wrote it

Fires will burn this evening
burn the dry husks of the corn
and I will learn to read

Sheep will wait by the trough
for they know corn's feature, corn's humility

corn's dichten

grain's

granite too

4) Theatre of the Stones that Ran (Fontao, 1943)

At night in the valley of penedos erguidos
a glint of wolfram

the uncles' job at night
to touch the glint of wolfram

wolfram brought riches for all in Fontao
they all had jobs then in Fontao
their nation was "neutral"
communism "vanquished"

They knew what night meant

the uncles mined a glint in the river's course
and stood up in the water
at night they worked each with two hands of xeo
and stood up in the water
climbed out of the river with the wolfram

penedos erguidos
human uncles, someday
and they ran

5) Theatre of the Confluence (A Carixa)

A little river and a big river
the story of the bronchials
Some of earth's heartbeat but not all

The water rose in the little river
and washed the big river away
Some of the lungs' telluric memory

The story of a rivermouth
and a confluence
From such a place you can hear the river
or you can breathe
but you have to choose or it chooses you

If it chooses you you are an asthmatic
Now you can live here forever
You can sit under the oak leaves and feel wet spray

The big river and the little river
The story of breath in a meander

The big river and the little river
A little story of leaves the river swept away

6) Theatre of the Peito (Santiso)

In a mother's arms lies a man
his skin is blue and his lips are blue
and his chest is a hayrick
flat with forks of blue
Perhaps he is dead, perhaps he is dreaming
perhaps he remembers the law has smote him down

he has shut his eyes
his eyes are open
his chest is a hayrick
His head is very tiny, bearded with thread

his head has the breadth of an onion
in a mother's arms
where is she carrying this onion:
its chest is so huge!
on the road above the house roofs:

why is this onion passing by?

7) Theatre of the Green Leira (Mandúa)

Is bad weather coming
how would we know
Is bad weather coming
call everyone

I am all alone cutting the grass or grain
cutting the wood I am alone
splitting it open carrying it to the crib
Call everyone, put the white table out in the yard
sharpen the knives the scythes
bring out the books now
sharpen the clock's knives too

where did we read any of this
my heart mad with beating
I might lie down here in this field before you arrive

call everyone
the flies are singing their hymnal hum hum ai ai
how would we know

the needles of the clock are cutting down the names of the hours

8) Theatre of the Pavement (Reboredo)

Nowhere yet has symbolism proven
adequate to the situation
Waiting for the boots to call out
from their stall by the door

Boots wet with river and a field's muck
Boots that touched a swollen sheep
lain there and a swollen yellow cat
lain there rain in its hair
little rivulets running down its body
its hair in wet swirls

Boots that found it there beside the road's calzada
A little grass grown round it far too soon
and no one to bring it to the earth again
though it touches the earth

and the boots touch the earth
that's all they do
touch the earth
that's all they do

from *No: a journal of the arts*

The Last Time I Saw Chris

◇   ◇   ◇

In Amagansett, for crying out loud, setting the arm of his French helpmeet
towards a funky-as-it-gets exhibit in the Crazy Monkey,
a cross-cut saw
in the window not quite making up for this not quite being Long Island
        Sound,
the gobs of tar
on his and his buddy's pants

suggesting they might have been willing participants
in some recent keel-hauling. Blown, too, the opportunity to meet
and greet an incipient Jack Tar
or wannabe grease-monkey
in an outhouse wired, for the love of mike, for sound.
When he turned away from me I could have sworn I saw

a woman on a see-saw
from the seventies, still flying a flag for the seventies. That's what was with
        the hotpants.
The politest way of putting it would be to say she and I'd been trying to
        sound
each other out, though it seemed unlikely ever the twain would meet.
She was just back from Benin. No monkey
business without an overcoat, for crying out loud. No losing the ship for a
        ha'p'orth of tar.

Not ship, I was treading water. *Sheep.* A sheep being the avatar
of no god we know of, always the best kind. For she was musing on an
        ancient saw
having to do with a monkey

and paying p(e)an(u)ts
to the guide, for the love of mike, who'd led her hunting trip. A hartebeest
        meet
summoned by a hartebeest bugle, a sound

that had barely the strength to resound
through the bush. Boots and saddles. The clench of Wright's Coal Tar
as she suddenly deemed it meet
to turn the other cheek, for crying out loud, looking back at me as if she saw
        that I foresaw
the needle-tracks just above the line of her pants
when her arms would set from years of firing up, as if I foresaw the monkey

on her back ("*les ans, mon ange, les ans manqués*"),
as if I might look forward from an era in which we were all still relatively
        sound
in wind and limb to an era of night sweats, gasps and pants,
for the love of mike, now threatening to tar
all of us, straight or gay, with the same brush, the god who oversaw
our not knowing of him yearning now to mete

our retribution as the hartebeest pants for cooling streams, *taratantara, taratan-*
        tara,
our breathing indistinguishable now from the sound of a saw
through the breast of a monkey, for crying out loud, through monkey- or
        other bush meat.

from *The New Yorker*

No Rewriting

◇　◇　◇

nobody's going to come in
and take my cup of money

sometimes the only no I have
is to reverse things

I agree. It's a good place to shit.

This morning it was summer
while I stayed in
I watched spring fade
I went out in chill fall
and walked my dog
in winters rectangles of trash
striking our face
the wind turning flags and banners
into danger
man the wind was big
in this fragmented
city

I want to be a part of something bigger than myself
not the university of california but it's a start
my dad was a gorilla

who did you think I would be

how do you spell univercity
it always looks cilly

I will think
I will read

I will wake up loving you and when I come home
I will love you.
Look I bought tickets for the movies for tomorrow night
I will buy you a hot dog then you know what

They didn't know I was so great
it was humbling
now it is fine

I sent her this email about the big awards
the paranoia I feel about all the award
winners
now I'm like king of the losers again
I said king king king

it's like genitals
I want to show you all these tiny parts

but I'm public public public

I went to the University of Massachusetts
and for all these years the city of New
York has given me a rent stabilization
grant

and now California golden state opens her
arms to us

come to mama

I wrote this poem twenty four years ago
but nobody saw it yet
so I'm safe

she said you are such a good boy

that morning I had just moved my car
today on the blue paper the hell's angels flag is
rolled like toilet paper, just a thin stream
of tattered flag thanks to the accident
of weather last night's wind

and I got back in bed and she called
I think the bridges will be closed
and everyone was screaming on the roof
there's another one
no she said I'm watching teevee
so I brought her up to the roof with me
and all my neighbors standing up there the whole block
like history and it flaming

and I met the poet Jason from the building next door
they've hit the pentagon someone yelled
and I went down to get some coffee
and when I came back one was down
wow I said to Jason
had I let go of you yet I can't remember
I went back to get some more
and none were left

I drink a lot less coffee now and I can sleep at night
but who could miss the flag like fourth of july
forever when they move the car
I think of it so much
when I ride over the manhattan bridge
on my bike or my car
when else do I look up
I never used to notice the towers

riding around Berlin This used to be a wall neighborhood
the wall was here, here, here
god they're haunted I thought
but where was it did I ever know
I just thought of it as 70s

and suppose it would've been nice to be a poet in residence
another grant I never got around to sending in

it was never out my window but I see it out there now

last night I thought about tripping
and the way the fags had yellow canvas deck chairs
and it was labor day and everyone was gone
it wasn't enough to sit on their furniture
at their little round table with the umbrella

we had this skid on the other side of the roof
they called it the dyke deck
and I remember lying there with our shirts off
so early in the morning
getting more and more sweet quarts of bud
writing with a soft pen
into the cheep industrial wood

more rebop

we thought fuck them
and threw the yellow deck chairs into the trees in the yard
they just hung there and we laughed and laughed
woke up thought oh no
there was a moment when they thought about evicting us
all the men

even the super Bill
who had some kind of anal cancer
an old marine who kept painting the foyer
you called it
the building's butt-hole

yellow and green
tan then brown
by the time he painted it horrible shiny silver
so bad when I was drunk
I thought what a goner
and yep he was dead soon

speaking of smells or halls tubes for living through

I think of Belanksy:

Little Girl

mainly I think you just have to take the loss into account
I don't care if you get it

Little Girl

holes in my memory

sticking my hands in my jeans
jackets
which ones have the torn pockets
I repaired
and where do I put my keys
now
which pants am I in
do I remember them?

the bread must be saved
wrapped, protected
from age
because I am poor

and how am I to dress my flesh
if I'm not poor
anymore
how can I protect me from rotting
how can I allow

buy a new loaf every day
throw it away
wildly fresh

Belansky who stunk
who never went out
hermit with a beard

and the stink poured when he opened
his door

little girl
go to the store for me
to buy baloney
and raisin bread
and two quarts of milk
for years
and keep the change

little girl

I'm 28
35
forty even forty
while he was still alive
some days walking really
slow past his door
I even knocked
I was so broke
I needed his forty cents

the day his stinky apartment was empty
now for years
the clean old man his brother
where were you all this time
when your brother had a beard
came to New York for something
grew inside here

from *Mississippi Review*

State of the Union

from *Alma, or the Dead Women*

◊   ◊   ◊

and when she. so the novel. glistens in all its propriety. and then he.
no it was where i spied no one knows any doves. and the cool
features of no one blue as the sky, which i've been studying. you are,
were you, that time. i don't have it's in my body. hemmed in by if the
all-powerful, but they're cliché inscribed. on the hemming-in wall.
a not very spectacular magpies' nest. it is a meeting in a familiar.
elections. she's not my friend; and will now introduce the two
strippers. if i'd known you'd wanted them last time, for i am the one
who can get them for you. and they're politics. because these two
strippers show you. i hear he's going to ask unwed mothers to marry.
the state of the union, is strippers in green g-strings. they were hired
by a blonde woman in makeup. because if you'd just said you didn't
need a speech. a poet is getting nervous: shouldn't we greet? look he's
here. why is the president so popular? because he is vicious. what
does that say about every other he will kiss the strippers. he will
make them turn into words: i am a man of honor. and what am i but a
servant girl? every citizen of small income. i have not hated so before.
i could hate this novel. i participate. i read the author applauded for he
has the ball. it is all one politics sports. you don't break it, because it
kisses you. the prompt money loves the exact one change from
another way of doing the same thing. so if you tell that story i have
run bleeding. all over myself. your talent to serve the state of the
union. in an elegy of it or in celebration of some kind autonomous
life. he's gone to be wed to another. term. he is unremarkably. once i
became this age the poem said he had sunk it. this is ignorance of how
many dark ships. i search the deep grave that no novel could come,
for the sleep can be told, in painful sounds he doesn't. to obliterate a

mind, that almost doesn't exist, its cruelty a reflex, but the novel believes in society. applauded these strippers green he would have to know a locution. it is requested that he not be opposed, but in the country i've entered i don't know the grammary. i use more than one to try. cruel death, my low. you wrote of the buried but without recognition. because at your table, the hollow present your talent. slowly the words arose and drank the wine of the wife. so many referees. could only know. so they ask everyone who thinks yes. in the winding sheets the nation owns. they have begged him to present strippers, and one began one's career that way. the vileness of so many i could not count. yet when i say "evil," it is not permitted. if it is his word. as if they owned them. or as if he could not be evil, even if his actions. because he's so popular. what does that say about novel, which requests living as. continuous approbation of country connecting people into time, so that they can be connected. by fingers intertwining all over the one countree, of peristaltic motion. it follows. and the dove thrashers a black list of unmattering. this is the state of the union. well-poised to explain. the state of the union is strippers. because starting with strippers the lime light leprous. and it is accepted. what you accept. what you have accepted. genitals.

from *Columbia Poetry Review*

Blue Collar Holiday

◊ ◊ ◊

And if I feel like a woman looming over Lautrec
With water weight & panties and murderous fuchsia underfoot,
Those dying balloons on Job's Lane sag around like saline breast implants
And pineal sunbeams sneak through my hair
Dirty but focused as screwy detectives or Plexiglas.
I go to pieces in my adolescent pine
Amid blackheads, seltzer, a cold front
Falling into a decline
Like ladies on the prairies used to . . .
In the kleig-lit house with the deodorant cakes in the upstairs johns
And the foam core ass on "Bad Secretary" in the living room
And the foam core bird paintings in the kleig-lit kitchen
Warm & endangered as an Orca whale float,
Pollen & Coronas, in the foggy autumn
And the thin nude branches all snow-furred
Like an X ray of infant bronchitis. Wrist-slitting stuff.
My honey chapstick stinks of piss & menstrual sharkfear
But like the alpha male in brownie troops ankled in mud,
I sit tight, coping, & spit. The Mormons taught me
To have fortitude when I am in the right & right now
I stand stalwart as lung-colored support hose
In a French sex & death-er for readers under twelve.
My indian name is "Little Hard-Core." I yank on a blue collar
Since we have so many blue collar holidays,
Salute myself for alpinism—just being high really
& degrees of cousinage even misty like this.

from *Hanging Loose, Exquisite Corpse*, and *Jacket*

DANIELLE PAFUNDA

RSVP

◇   ◇   ◇

Don't invite me to your pity party.
Don't call me up on your pity party line
and invite me over for punch and cookies.
I won't come. I won't come
with a pretty pity present. I won't
put on my pity party dress with the special
ribbon in my pity pony tail. I won't play
pity pin the tail on the donkey,
or dance to pity pop music. I don't care
if the captain of the football team
and the whole pity pep squad are coming.

I don't care if your mother made her special
pineapple upside-down pity or your father plans
to grill pity pups and hamburgers. Not even
if you have an exotic pity parrot that says
Polly want some pity, or if you have the newest
model Pontiac Pity that we can drive around in.
Head up to the hills, watch the sun set
and the bright lights of the big pity turn on.

It's your party, and you know what that means,
but it's not my style. You know what I always say.
I say, *kill the people*, and *never let 'em see you sweat*.
I always say *this party's for the birds*,
and *who invited you, anyway, pal?*

from *Pleiades*

Real Toads

◊   ◊   ◊

He got up to play in the partable

terrible vision. I don't think I can fall asleep
if the door is open, do you? Finally,

we bridge to word it, ticking off our

trues. Sly by sly, backs up against
the all, a rational awe keeling. A thirst

bell sounded in the distress, we

scat dawn on the then monstrous. Verily
showy, the harness gives say. I'm

rowing out to get flume flesh bare,

order a furl to quiver me a good lushing,

swap acquired state sanctioned
for swarm, flare a now starry.

He shrugs, Wet ever.

from *La Petite Zine*

Here 2

◊　◊　◊

Fact: the cordially hated present
finally emerged from its dressing gown for good
the morning Proust dipped his Krispy Kreme into Kafka's coffee
and the whole market for stable meaning collapsed,
exposing me to the gravity of the moment, dinky,
but strong enough, apparently,
to pull me out of the family tree, family of man,
American consumer army family, no parachute

but the poetry map I'd stitched together
back in the uncounted days from pages flying into the future,
written or read, who cared,
here be epics,
here be epiphanies,
here be state of the art oceanic marginalities,
last month the Gross Poetic Product showed a modest increase,
continuing the trend from the dawn of history,

but now writing as I thought I knew it
has ripped open, I've gained weight, apparently,
body lurking in the weeds all the while, its endless voiceovers
more familiar by now than memory,

read by soothing Furies looking straight out at the camera,
late breaking faces making eye contact
out of the mask of uniform intelligence, brisk concern, it's in the contract,
mouths fully employed, nimble with the universal accent,
undisturbed by closeups of local carnage,
datelines and places crawling slavishly beneath,

we the media, all other pronouns confiscated,
and there's no way to turn this off,
the mute button's broken, like all the others,
so much for the thought that the remote was autonomous, mine,
that I could write
and it would do the rest,

this must be the work of History, Today's Date,
this morning's neural releases,
the tiny dreams,
the plans, ever-huger, are these the powers?
tangled in their tenses, entrapped, embedded, what I write,
wrote, you read, will read,
with just an is or two in between
separating making from made, broken from breaking open,

hardly enough,
but that's what there is to work with,
sirens blasting away, ignore them at the risk of enchantment,
and what's the opposite of that? and where else would it put us?
and before the question mark touches down Echo has answered,
Yes, we know, knowledge
echoes from the tapes so thoughtfully
that we know what we think
and without pause

we're back
in the loop, the world before us in all directions,
asking only for our spontaneous ignorance,
giftwrapped with gold ribbons, bows of burning desire,
a present
with a person inside,
personally monogrammed, cut, it's a wrap,
the irony will never be fresher, the studied refusals of cliche more intense,
those frames, these happy coincidental hours

with in and out on the same page,
vale and dale rolling in unison,
forests dancing onto boxcars, autonomous trunks trundled toward utopia,
at least that's what each machined length is told

at graduation, Pleistocene entailments smoking up the scenery,
pissing away the rivers, nowhere to rest
for the weary, or the bored, or the teary,

there are no final surfaces, on earth, in dreams,
no bright pages on which to fix the just sentences,
writing on water turns out to be a play on words,
a pun that only works
because inside a language
everything sounds more or less the same,

the Federal Building
says Federal Building on the outside
and the cement is fine with it, apparently,
so why, legibility wonders, does meaning have to be such a pill?
how many tons of therapy will it take
just to exit the revolving door, to stand on the corner,

amid the growing suspicion
that the problem is one of basic structure,
that the mind's infoliations are only crude links
lashing the sea to its names
without prior consent, or even notice,
a kind of invasion you might say,

even though intelligibility knows it's for the best,
articulation and pleasure will follow,
they already do, don't they?
frisking around the heels of power,
but there's a certain unease, an itch
that anxious stares from even the best dogs can't scratch,
a terror that being emperor in no matter how many other brains
can't squash, no way can enough satisfaction fit inside
a single body, even if it swallows every good thing on the horizon,

novelty all day and mood music all through the night,
plus the fantasy powers, because when they give you
the keys to Philadelphia and the people who live here,
you'll find, on the same chain, the keys to Baghdad
and the bodies in the bunkers of the Federal Buildings there,

but if these keys open any line of credible inquiry,
the small print says
there is no more sleep, no more awakening,
Surrealism is was
the last gasp of that logic,
its snores issuing in apnean revolt,

leaving volcanic fragments the curators shelve, aroused but careful,
in ever sharper catalogs, signals for the bidding
to go a little crazy, rediscover its beliefs,
relive foundational erotic breakthroughs,
but the gavel hardly makes a dent, the openings closed long ago,
the niches are decades deep, fuzzy light sifts down
on the waxy subjectivities, cooling, cool, cold,

a singular stylus would be good,
but there's only so much time to press into the material,
and only so much material to go around,
which creates distortions of course, but you're not?
so amid the proclamations of perfected desire
better hold on to your donut
or you'll be fed to the equals signs

from *DCPoetry Anthology 2003*

Pleasure

◇ ◇ ◇

This far in—
where to say *the sea*
and mean *impossible*

makes sense,
why not—you can
almost forget

what brought you here,
the water it started with,
a life that has sometimes (admit

this much) seemed mostly
an only half-wanted because
finally unruly

animal you'd once hoped
to change by changing
its name: from *If Only* to

How Did I
to *In Spite of Everything*—
but nothing sticks, that doesn't

have to. Not memory;
not the naming—which, if a form of
remembering, is also

a form of *to own,* possession,
whose lineage
shifts never: traced

far enough, past hope, back across
belief, it ends always
at desire—without which

would there have been
imagination, would
there be folly,

one spreading itself
like a bay tree, the other
a green olive tree in the house

of God?
This far in, sky
is everything. Clouds cross it

like ships,
sheer will, regret
itself cut abruptly

loose. Lovely, when you say so,
—and when you don't.
It was never for you.

from *Tin House*

Samba

◊   ◊   ◊

The Hudson's not a river but an estuary. Palisades Park
Was a hit, then a jingle, or was it the other way round?

What's the difference? Or is it a difference O City of
Makers, among measures of freedom & commerce? It is

So a river because it is The Hudson River. In the same
Restaurant where Dick Powell ate with Veronica Lake,

Pacino shoots Hayden in the forehead & he falls face first
Into his spaghetti—making the place still more desirable to

Us from across the River & beyond, stunned too by live
Reindeer at Bloomie's. Donder & Blixen are caribou.

On the screen an old Eskimo with a caribou-bone needle
And thread of caribou sinew stitches together a raincoat

From strips of caribou gut. "You make use of every part
Of the caribou?"—the filmmaker's voice. The old guy

Smiles answering in Inuit while we wait for the subtitle—
"Everything but the shit!"—laughing as he keeps sewing:

Like a City answer, that profane assurance & fatalism.
A Canal herbalist might sell tincture of caribou droppings

For your cancer or your orchids. City of healers & cheaters.
Streets of sowers & killers, weavers & reapers. In front of

"Goan Foods" the vendor of girly lighters & bargain
CDs is dickering with his customer. They were born on

Different continents & the CD is not shit, it is the many-
Rooted music of the great Brazilian, Caetano Veloso.

from *The Threepenny Review*

In the First Circle
of Limbo

◇ ◇ ◇

Liberate me,
          Muse,
from this encirclement
          of categories.
Your themes
          are plein-air
endless
          sad.
Put some wit
          and compassion
into this pen!

from *American Poetry Review*

ED ROBERSON

Ideas Gray Suits
Bowler Hats Baal

◊   ◊   ◊

Adventure somehow decides to bypass all the already
for future release   I attended the last

a graceful request to the quiet you could sense
a scrappy sharing of their account of the music behind them

notational stirrings of a season slower than temperature
a delicate four days up her husky voice   History

a lesson as wearying as it is perpetual
A pruning   no matter how falsifying   of its real complexity

the lighting always perfect for its becoming extinct
just as soup begins simply and innocently   poor

but the mind is always filled with so many ideas
gray suits and bowler hats lifting silently the last

century   and this
jumping in flames from a roaring height for a fooled god

and his cow disease of long rotted enemies
not babel   people driven mad by the silences

they think into
empty voices

viciously ancient idol cow
disease of long rotted enemies

from *Chicago Review*

The 3D Matchmove Artist

◊　◊　◊

Please remove that tendril from my armrest
stated Professor Armitage matter-of-factly
as the blizzard picked up the chalet

Like a mountebank emptying the contents
of a bureau drawer onto the floor at the feet
of a girl clutching an atomizer

Like the last dendrite on a neural network
this swirling motion produces a hazy view
of Lake Toehold up ahead on the right

Remove your glasses
the chipped, striated containment walls
slip shivering into the slotted earth

A jarring sensation leaves us speechless
for a moment, then Will Smith utters
another *mot juice* and all hell

Breaks for lunch it's just another
day at the office only this time
the brain boys bought bread shoes

So it's gonna be a cakewalk
no biggee, XYZ chromosomes
should be interesting, we'll see, hello!

Standard sensation meter brackets
flashing somewhere across the bridge
and if you don't have a spoon

Don't look here for a view
the ice will just cream all over you
latency barometer zero

Your place per night
fantasy replacing extracurriculars
in the wingnut lounge

You really ought to do something about those tables
said the stars
and for a moment I believed them

from *DCPoetry Anthology 2003*

the story

◇　◇　◇

1.

it was and on was so
felt my saying myself could so
but or he was I in
in anymore was happening at come
to my me kept you way
across be put then me things
so we came and all him
in the feel saying me

2.

was a we the my big
terrible voice no saying and fast
why what wasn't happening loud the
the in my or all back
say breast how saying are the
your inside me two all like
I were I my but on
Ohio earth so this

3.

a friend were bed friend on
small the why no I it
wasn't if stopping in enough hallway
hallway the body maybe and I'm
his and beautiful oh like streetlight
body your finger then the when
wondered doing figured body where the
in and small years

4.

saturday it in I his my
and one couldn't or was was
he he anyway the to and
and hallway when I when not
hands he I G-d an comes
I body inside three while you're
if and it was was bed
the why and later

5.

and was my thought hands body
where that I maybe saying white
hearing was and hallway be who
why and this wasn't did sure
were was was oh angel in
need so my then saying making
that's when must there I in
United States do have he

6.

he late room he were which
was was hear I it noise
me and what was heard was
wasn't where was there I now
on telling the G-d the shining
to he vagina straddled loving love
what I be after under Kent
on I trouble raped

From *PMS*

JENNIFER SCAPPETTONE

III

◇   ◇   ◇

i.

                    pray you I pray on   new
  dogwood   on this our miscellaneous   eyes
the root of which   being   today country
we've not idea   the color was part of it   having being
union random   I was ok then   bohemian

I conjure you to   that hint of cleavage   one's own
this, understand,   teardrop cut from a dress   personal
us greys   in the office   world
& not of New England,   that convention   once my choices yours

wasn't raised   the color of my mother   then it was the new
that way it's   my foster   you wanted it had it
the unspoken   my abandon   I still don't know what happened
Neapolitan   following abandon   cruxes I can't pronounce
foundation of street abandon   tattooed heart   *trouver* a whole lifelink
that singing   initial branded   to this jazz
the nonarticulate   I was so sure   that acts me
that my inheritance   you're all the same   silence
a legion of shut mouths you women in writing   it's the tangle of things
it's not the right time   masking this   I've always loved you

every thing needs sewing   isn't her isn't me authored   I don't want to break
but they're all lined up   now, on a plane   now I couldn't
it's all determined   —Paris, New Orleans—   Hong Kong
and no   put the voice in a box   don't know when
                      lock it   soon
yell   evermore   some weekends

California maybe
I don't know
(knots)
(vague determination)
listen to me.
it's just what's right
It has to be

& babies will fill that hollow
bliss I promise
just listen to Al Green
& don't make me rip the rearview
mirrordown.
I'm tired just let me rest,
light for me just once
No surrogate

no future
not a miring in the past
connecting it,
I mean all that
these notions are halfbaked understand
don't hold me to them
It just deserves a lot that's what

i. (across)

It's the opera in the sky.
It's the cookie I keep for you always.
It's the alley of olives on the way home. The cured.
The wind kicking up around our form.
That lavender envelope of hours above the plain.
It's the topography of Venice.
An evening I hated you by the wharf.
It's the dead one rose.
It's the bowler & dress of stars I bore around you.
(A decade ago in a snapshot aimed at the ceiling.)
It's the distance of a screen.
Greed humane. (Okay kill it couldn't hold you) Still
It's the way I loved you.

from *Boston Review*

Love Song

◇　◇　◇

I shaved my legs a second time,
Lagoon approaching the sublime,
To cast a moonlight spell on you.
TriBeCa was Tahiti, too.

I know I never was on time.
I was downloading the sublime
To cast a moonlight spell on you.
TriBeCa was Tahiti, too.

The melanoma on my skin
Resumes what's wrong with me within.
My outside is my active twin.
Disease I'm repetitious in.

The sun gives life but it destroys.
It burns the skin of girls and boys.
I cover up to block the day.
I also do so when it's gray.

The sunlight doesn't go away.
It causes cancer while they play.
Pre-cancerous will turn out bad.
I had an ice pick for a dad.

A womanizing father, he's
The first life-threatening disease.
His narcissistic daughter tried
To be his daughter but he died.

The richest man in Delaware
Died steeplechasing, debonair.
One company of ours made napalm.
That womanizing ice pick's gray calm

Died steeplechasing in a chair,
The jockey underneath the mare.
She posted and she posted and
Quite suddenly he tried to stand

And had a heart attack and died,
The ice pick jockey's final ride.
The heart attack had not been planned.
He saw my eyes and tried to stand.

My satin skin becomes the coffin
The taxidermist got it off in.
He stuffed me, made me lifelike. Fatten
My corpse in satin in Manhattan!

My body was flash-frozen. God,
I am a person who is odd.
I am the ocean and the air.
I'm acting out. I cut my hair.

You like the way I do things, neat
Combined with craziness and heat.
My ninety-eight point six degrees,
Warehousing decades of deep freeze,

Can burst out curls and then refreeze
And have to go to bed but please
Don't cure me. Sickness is my me.
My terror was you'd set me free.

My shrink admired you. He could see.
Sex got me buzzing like a bee
With Parkinson's! Catastrophe
Had slaughtered flowers on the tree.

My paranoia was revived.
I love it downtown and survived.
I loved downtown till the attack.
Love Heimlich'd me and brought me back.

You brought me life, glued pollen on
My sunblock. Happy days are gone
Again. My credit cards drip honey.
The tabloids dubbed me *Maid of Money*.

Front-page divorce is such a bore.
I loathed the drama they adore.
You didn't love me for my money.
You made the stormy days seem sunny.

from *Fence* and *Harper's*

A Burning Interior

◊   ◊   ◊

1.

of a copy of nothing
or more precisely a series
of xerox sketches of
burning interior-exteriors
No one guesses in that rotted century
not nothing but grey hints in
crayon flecks for bitter
perspective produced by a reproductive
machine looking at itself as usual
askance all the black windows blur
into a recessive landscape of
secondaries O like the gate into your flowers
forty-seven tulips shy of counting
then expanding into the scandalous
world since there is one
to die quickly in color in the tub
like Marat smiling and stabbed near the name of art

not Skelton to the Present but the child's future
from skeleton to the President
in this no-place
for any angel's perverb ("the hole in my heart leads to the hole
that is God—which is deeper")
next modulating with words "grey and pink
always work" when the
bedroom doesn't the Tolstoyan hanging

in the sonata of bilingual espressivo
repercussions of a hymn to
death in variations of an unearthed
happiness in lieu of rondo
when the circle was smashed by the hymn
(no one deserves better to leave
that model of a house) where you say
I will be kept crucially updated
but the undated "soul" held together
as if by black hinges or
murdered city's black snow I cannot see
But I see the pages of your books
opening wildly like the unfinished tulips
the excess and potlatch of the sun
Return, return to me
lost student of the plague

2.

Sinking, below the star-several harps
of evening, in one distant garden,
the new poem, twisted from the skin of the old whining birch—
Perhaps I am also dedicated to an angel's memory
her long black hair collected in my bed.
Now the youngest poet cries. I love countdowns! I love
the last few seconds of joy!
But the old poet knows the error in transcription
is correct: Nirvana is some sorrow.
Remember our last hacked Ariels
lie ruined in their melody. Two poems, folded, twisted together.
The earliest song: Because you have joined me
this great tree was felled. Is it worthless?
Because you have joined
never to leave again
spring has become the spring I had hoped for
and this crooked pebble is singing in the forest.
But the new poem, the winter flower, is not sweet.

3.

In another world, listening to a Yemenite dump
Dreaming of Jerusalem our popular flesh,
A sleeper a singer whose name is a triple pun
A language where skin would be light,
It all sounds like the king's first love.
But in this world we sit to translate.
God splits and the blind man's reference
Ends like the war ever not quite.
As we forget the grammar we are of red clay, an idiot.
The suppliants approach, on the field of untranslatable force.
Simone says nothing but: Poetry
More difficult than mathematics, as I warned you.
And the old poets, and the books appear themselves,
Holiness in Sin, that enraged Gershom—the doubled books
And the body's words: Blessed is He who created the creation.
Blessed are they who created the blessing.

4.

When a poet is weak,
like a broken microphone,
he still has some power,
indicated by a red light.

The weak poet
is fixed to the wall
like an ordinary light.

Dependent and dismal by turns,
he is a nominalist
and a razor blade
and a light

And the demons cry,
Cast him from the kingdom
for a copy of a copy!

Remove him
like the women who supported the temple—
slaves too free and alive.
His similes are ingenious, like science among lovers.

My friend, however early
you called, you had come
too late, again.

The weak poet
has not gone grey
but his sacrificed similes
lead nowhere.

And his I is like any other word
in the newspaper and he is cut up
like fashion.

Each window was seductive,
but even his diseases could be cured.
Your low voice alone
is major like a skepticism.

We had forgotten
the place and the stories,
and the fiery method, too familiar, too distant.

We had memorized the poems,
but only for prison.
With the first new year celebrated in chaos
above the red waters of Paradise.

Where a clayey groom
hears the bride's voice
like a stronger world—

Sound is all
a snake can do—
and charming sense
and strangeness

Now the old poet
loses his voice like a garden.
But finds it again, like a street in a garden.

In the injured house
made of local sun and stone—
In the city of numbers
which everyone counts and hates and wants—

We could read together in a dark city garden,
scribbling with language over
screens like lips, scribbling the first mistranslations.

5.

Who but he
Would talk to a teapot
She deposed in a dream
Who but he

But that's what a poet I replied
Does His occupation Rosemarie
He talks to a teapot
And a teapot talks back to him

What do you think writing unity
Is The poet is never alone
Talking at night to a teapot
The teapot talks back to him

He wrote six-foot poems
She received the letters
And put them in order ceaselessly
But how do we know the order

In which he received them (him) for real
Out of time like out of stamps
Torn time so funny so unfunny like a zebra
Kicking and almost killing you my mother

The poet takes a day off*
Never to work with the glass tower master
No more than he hears birds in his sleep
An ordinary goose goes squawking across the parking lot

The poet is photographed like a baby in a womb
The poet talks but not alone to the teapot
And it all sings (back to him)
It the your you speaks back to him

O simple world
It talks back to him
Even a goose though common
In time

Though aggressive and fat
In New Jersey
Beautifully bends its neck
In fog to speak

6.

They were right who inveighed against
the voice,
too sexual an organ
the rabbis those laryngologists
those who stopped a doctor
by their side like a singer
who refused to listen

*He works and you work and I
There is only one day off
There is no day off
For a bug in a forest. Recommence

The footnote hangs
Like hair in space
Hair that became over time
A blue dolphin

and put a wall where voice had been
they died the lover of branches
of fire of the tape recorder used for good or ill your burning hair

If we were blind
and if we were known to listen
we would find one another
by your voice alone
(what you loved or Lilith loved was you and yes and permission)
and we are blind

7.

Our father
restless afraid of death
would say You will rest
when you're dead

Perhaps not!
And: Practice or you'll eat
in the garage
with the dog

Dead as the light
bulb is living still
A secret for the light bulb
is the nap

of broken music
There are some veins
in brown plaster
But the world emits

a little light
You wore cereal boxes
as a belt
I wore electric light

as another mistake
The search continued
for more veins and
a dented skull

This too had a pedestal
or place
or base or double
door or triple tomb.

8.

Long live the instant
long live the king and queen
killers in their vaccary
Long live
the tour around the periplus
with walkie-talkies in a drift
Long live a city by a destroyed lake
and simple water-clocks
Long live the word dark
the poet who was once a whiz
and a concert-master
art historian of
hurries desperately and is now
just a poet

Long live the double foyer
of your undestroyed body
and our bed made out of the oaken earth
Long live such displacements
as are possible in the skena
of lack of recognition
Long live the unweaving
Long live the pierced son
Long live the middle-aged
sagging home from oblivion
to other caves
Long live the catachresis

of our lives in New Jersey
and Troy and in wandering eraser fluid
and books of many naked devices
Long live the interruption
of this fragile art

And long live it
when the sun beats
on a living shelter
and clarifies each blade
and the heavenly breasts
stand out to be sucked
and the earth bursts

9.

Out of being torn apart
comes art.

Out of being split in two
comes me and you. HA HA!

Out of being torn in three
comes a logical poetry. (She laughed but not at poetry.)

Out of the essential mistranslation
emerges an illegitimate nation.

Better she said the enraged
than the impotent slave sunk in the Bay.

Out of being split into thirteen parts
comes the eccentric knowledge of "hearts."

(Out of being torn at all
comes the poor-rich rhyme of not knowing, after all.)

And out of this war, of having fought
comes thinking, comes thought.

10.

He deduced from all aesthetics
in small boldface with shining serifs:
"He got nothing"
Translated from the Norwegian:
"Pleasure is so difficult,
like tennis, like music,
sorrow is so sly, so easy."
He wept all over the dream.
Received the dream-letter:
"Forgive me for (you) using you
It jolts me to think of uh it—"
Theology had apologized.
At the old grammar school, at the beginning,
father exploded. A critic wrote
"I'm not much on textures,
dreams, verbal links;
and not very big on satire, either."
Thank you for liking the last line the subject on fire
or fire in the photograph.

11.

Blessed is the architect of the removed structures
Blessed is the structure that weathers in spring snow like lies
Blessed is the crystal that leaps out of the matrix like a fool
And blessed is the school

Blessed factures
Blessed like spring snow
Blessed like a fool
And burnt book

Is the school a structure or weather
Or a lie like spring snow
And is the matrix leaping also like a fool
And is the book built or burnt?

Blessed is the removed
Blessed too the inlay like spring
Blessed is the tiger of the matrix like a found fool
And blessed the unbuilt like a book

Blessed is the architect who survives all removal
Blessed is the trapped structure like a gift
Blessed is the crystal fool
And blessed is the school

Blessed is the cut and the cry
Blessed the body of the patient in spring snow like lies
Blessed is the crystal stepping out of the matrix like a fool
And blessed is a burning book

Blessed is the anchorite and the architect in the dark smudge
Blessed is the remover bending to remove
Blessed is the folly leaping out of matrix
And blessed is the empty center

Blessed burning structures
Blessed like snowy spring
Blessed cry blessed in the matrix like a cut fool
And blessed each unlit book

Blessed is the architect of the removed cut
Blessed the structures that weather in lies like spring snow
Blessed is the crystal that leaps out of the matrix like a fool
And blessed is the school, like a burning library

Old new prayer
Old new song
Blessed is the crystal and the cry and the matrix like a painting fool
And blessed is the school

from *SHINY*

Compliance Engineering

from *VOG*

◊ ◊ ◊

Our true form is the blurb.
Full moon in a clear December sky
on page 215 of my notebook.
Ice cream machine
rejects my crumpled dollar.
Stairwell dark behind the fire doors.
When this you recall, take care
not to stumble (your rime here
makes us what to cheer)
on all that is the case.
In Philly, sleeveless t-shirts
are called "wife-beaters."
Pale grey of the leafless woods.
Architect's signature
is the pink tile bath.
Small plane wobbles
as it glides
into rural airstrip.
Toyotathon: whoda thunk?
Close reading: Pop-up Video
is not that. What
you get if you see
stranger as parallel to danger.
A toy train endlessly circles
the table-top track.
One drawer in the kitchen
just for rubber bands.

Waldo's evil Other: Odlaw.
The wrong pen here
because the right one is missing,
the ink does not sink in
but rests atop the paper's grain,
a gleam in the grease of it, clots
whenever the line changes direction.
A small gazebo constructed over an old well
and next door a utility substation,
sheer red brick block.
Last house in these woods
to leave the Christmas lights on
outdoors through the night.
Paintings purchased entirely for their frames
so he becomes a constructor of margins
to build a "house" with no right angles.
Antithetical to reason, to contemplation,
is called the Discovery Zone.
Holding a potato chip with both hands.
The stamp on your palm visible
by means of a special light.
Weighted prosody of cartoon. Outbreaks
migrate from species to species
in search of the perfect host.
The alarmed door sounds: young workers
in identical t-shirts stampede
toward the exit. Language
poetry understood
as a problem of nostalgia
(Tarkovsky imitates Antonioni).
At dawn, tufted titmice and black-capped
chickadees approach the feeder in groups,
taking turns in rapid succession,
lone cardinal watches from a branch,
squirrels beneath waiting for the dropped seed.
Small fluorescent night-light for the bathroom
my son calls "rectangular moon."
Lines link lives like words,
glances, an embrace, capable
entirely of administration, deceit,

want, need, the long sigh,
meaning evident to no one.
Pirbuterol acetate
inhalation aerosol
puffer inserted
into the mouth: breathe deeply
counting slowly to twenty.
Downy woodpecker taps at the oak.
Geometric passion:
he looks just like his web site.

from *Antennae*

Song of the Ransom
of the Dark

◇   ◇   ◇

A neural, feral fix on the beautiful movie face
        I went to Vietnam to adopt a kid
like a baby bird imprinted to the worst affliction, havoc, holocaust
        I wanted meaning in my life
from my seat in the dark while I sipped a Coke
        Poetry had failed me
a movie set, a rear projection, junk
        slowly poetry had failed me
it seems. It's where the conversation took place
        first as grace, then as skin, then
a back and forth like flame. It is where love came from
        as woman as terminal being
as fetish—a thigh, a foot in heels—all of what we wanted
        plucked up again and woven
fatality and church and commodity—something about to burst
        the way it's supposed to work, to purl and circle
into my lap from my purchase in
        you like the mats and baskets of the country
a plush paranoia of the glance
        the squat huts and women's carrying in the rain
of horror or color in our *Wizard of Oz*
        that's still the third world
or *Apocalypse Now Redux*, redux
        and corrupt as if America wasn't
hard to horrify, hard to please
        everyone who speaks my language has bad teeth and

I can't remember in the film why in the first place
a hand out that wants to be greased
the government hired Ingrid Bergman
In the first place what's the word for want
but I remember the head lights and the curve
or want to have where have = pay = name =
the fragment of music, the set of keys
crime = proof of my desperation
the set of keys like coins or slow rain
then I enter a dark room
and a moment when the black white
like a latecomer to a movie
faces are all there are
where there's a table with a can of Coke
an infinitely prolonged walk up the stairways
and a bare bulb that's from a torture scene
dizzying and it's not the horror
I imagine—they say your mother was an American
but the pleasure that can be found daily
and I am broken down in front of
the infinitely prolonged kiss
the small boned men and I must insist
encircling glances, tracking shots, arabesques
in spite of it all I am fit to mother
the one dialect of shadow and the war, the girl,
all this because of the failure of
the eye dilated

from *POOL*

They're Putting
a New Door In

◊   ◊   ◊

Brian's new shoes. She asked me of his whereabouts. They're putting a new door in.

CCI. They're putting a new door in. Impersonating an officer.

They're putting a new door in. Feliz Navidada. My watch continues to stop: self-identity.

> I break,
> WFMU.
> Margin time,
> the steaming metropolis
> wakes
> at 8 am
> with dry lips.
> I couldn't take my eyes off the ball.

Papers on her head. Like a crown of spring thorns. They're putting a new door in.

This is only the third poem I've written in 2001. And probably the last one. The other two went like this:

It hit with the farce of an atom bomb.
If there are no animals on Mars, is there anything that could classify as "shit."

People are like ciphers. They say this, they say that.
Private life is a social experiment.
The French: an impatience with secular explanations.
Writing. Boiling potatoes.
Everybody's pride is hurt.

And:

Footfalls, bubblebaths.
Hezbollah and hot dogs.
Be sure to add these Tones of War
to your arsenal of meters.

from *Boston Review*

Dog That I Am

◇　◇　◇

I sing for the similarity and I moan for
the face, dog that I am, whippet that I was,
her face of exhaustion, lines in her forehead, her hair
uncombed and unbrushed, the wind in her eyes, she could be
from Thrace, from Denmark, I could be from Rome
waiting for her command, I could be from
Egypt and dogging her and I could be from
Spain, a silky wearing a sweater and she with
a scarf at her throat and another one over her mouth
bending to hold my face up, wearing a herring-bone
overcoat with deep pockets and buttons
circa 1940, 1950 with
black westies on her feet and neat little
lapets at the top, the neighborhood of Skinker
near a birch tree, only an accident,
just a mistake—I scream outright at the likeness.

from *Lyric*

La Florida

◇   ◇   ◇

Lugubrious days pass with the amplitude of manatees,
hibiscus unfold their smiling vortex to confused bees,

somewhere near turkey point a crocodile grows a foot
by the day, tourists mistake the big ones for logs,

anhingas play Jesus on the Spanish moss-riddled branches
of oaks and junipers, crucified in the sun. Feral Quaker

parrots build nests high up in the banyan trees. Orchids,
capuchin monkeys loosed from an animal distributor

warehouse, memories of the bearded lady and the lizard
man, retired now in Palatka, holding court in the shade

of a parasol by their trailer. Russian midgets, rockets
shot into the eye of the moon, this magic of fireflies

zapping their phosphorescence in the night air, jasmine,
gardenia—somewhere a man barbecues four-inch-thick steaks

in a thing called the Green Egg. A firefighter, a player
of handball. When his son visits once a year from Vegas

he asks when will he return to Tampa, his home. Who isn't
lured by so much sun, heat? The permanence of weather—

or by the mystery of sun showers when the sky opens up
and pelts the earth with a momentary lapse of crying.

Right now, somewhere in the Everglades, a fish jumps
out of the water and into the mouth of an alligator.

Nobody's there to witness it, but it happens again and again.

from *New England Review*

ARTHUR SZE

Acanthus

◇   ◇   ◇

When you shut your eyes, you find a string
of mackerel tied by the tail over and across
the sloping street; pour water into *raki*
and watch it cloud into "lion's milk";
nibble smoked aubergine with yogurt;
point to red mullet on a platter of fish.
You catch the sound of dripping water,
squat to be near to the upside down Medusa
head at the column base in a cistern:
a drop of water splashes your forehead.
You note carved acanthus leaves, then
eighteen women in singular postures
of mourning along the sides of a sarcophagus;
turn, at a noise, to bright lights:
eighteen men and women in security shirts
swarm through the covered street,
search for heroin. You smell saffron,
cardamom, frankincense, cinnamon, ginger,
galingale, thyme, star anise, fennel:
open your eyes to leeches in a jar
half-filled with water—green powdered henna
in a box alongside white mulberries.
The bells around the necks of goats clink;
you run your fingers along the fragments
of terra-cotta pots built into the stone
walls of houses; blink at the beggar
whose foot has swollen to the size
of his head; stagger up to Athena's temple
by moonlight; sit on a broken column,

231

gaze out across the gulf to Lesbos,
where lights glimmer along the curve
of a bay. In waxing moonlight, the water
is riffled, argentine, into wide patches.
You ache at how passion is a tangle
of silk in your hands, shut your eyes,
unstring the silk in one continuous thread.

from *The Butcher Shop* and *Manoa*

Bounden Duty

◇　◇　◇

I got a call from the White House, from the
President himself, asking me if I'd do him a personal
favor. I like the President, so I said, "Sure, Mr.
President, anything you like." He said, "Just act
like nothing's going on. Act normal. That would
mean the world to me. Can you do that, Leon?" "Why,
sure, Mr. President, you've got it. Normal, that's
how I'm going to act. I won't let on, even if I'm
tortured," I said, immediately regretting that "tortured"
bit. He thanked me several times and hung up. I was
dying to tell someone that the President himself called
me, but I knew I couldn't. The sudden pressure to
act normal was killing me. And what was going on
anyway. I didn't know anything was going on. I
saw the President on TV yesterday. He was shaking
hands with a farmer. What if it wasn't really a
farmer? I needed to buy some milk, but suddenly
I was afraid to go out. I checked what I had on.
I looked "normal" to me, but maybe I looked more
like I was trying to be normal. That's pretty
suspicious. I opened the door and looked around.
What was going on? There was a car parked in front
of my car that I had never seen before, a car that
was trying to look normal, but I wasn't fooled.
If you need milk, you have to get milk, otherwise
people will think something's going on. I got into
my car and sped down the road. I could feel those
little radar guns popping behind every tree and bush,
but, apparently, they were under orders not to stop

me. I ran into Kirsten in the store. "Hey, what's going on, Leon?" she said. She had a very nice smile. I hated to lie to her. "Nothing's going on. Just getting milk for my cat," I said. "I didn't know you had a cat," she said. "I meant to say coffee. You're right, I don't have a cat. Sometimes I refer to my coffee as my cat. It's just a private joke. Sorry," I said. "Are you all right?" she asked. "Nothing's going on, Kirsten. I promise you. Everything is normal. The President shook hands with a farmer, a real farmer. Is that such a big deal?" I said. "I saw that," she said, "and that man was definitely not a farmer." "Yeah, I know," I said, feeling better.

from *American Poetry Review*

The Theorist
Has No Samba!

◇   ◇   ◇

there is a new instantism > a language of tangent =
tanguage > ambient funguage > there is a modern path
> invented through accidental spontaneity + of mock
language sport = fractured intelligentsillys > there
are sage athleticists + important children farmed out
to the furthest reaches of nowness > . . . > . . . >

I propose a New Instantism. Take spontaneousness out
of the ether and smack it into the throes of the wild
screaming bastard maggot that IS poetry! I propose a
New NEWness, where we refuse to comply by the aged
fumblings of mere MEANING and instead descend into
mere HEARING! I instigate a NEW failure of
listening . . . so we may one day walk hand in hand with
our own ears and say . . . THANK THE MIGHTY LOUD THAT I
MAY THANK THE MIGHTY LOUD THAT I MAY THANK THE MIGHTY
LOUD! I have a NEW Instantaety, a modern NEWness, a
post NOWism . . . I have a fear . . . of hiding this fear,
instead . . . I choose a revelry of failure, an opportune
dementia into the song of my pacifism.

Let's say we level expectation with implied tension.
The instant doubt appears, possibility appears next to it as a window.
What was thought to have clarity is now diffused by possibility.
Is possibility the goal . . . or only the instant before doubt?

The New Instantists will allow possibility room to
doubt itself . . . inventing a paranoia into the sleepless
monster that is this bastard maggot poetry. The New
Instantist will know that it takes a flat surface to
iron out procedure, that a wrinkled pair of favorite
pants will match an equally wrinkled ass . . . and mind.
That no matter how just or unjust the outcome . . . the
New Instantist will always be blamed for what has just
happened! Occurrence . . . being the signpost
for all things instant.

To what is now
And what is never then
To what has been
And what will never now
To things all thinging
And soon all soon'ing
To what is now
Instantly now

from *Van Gogh's Ear*

Meditatio Lectoris

◊　◊　◊

Caucus how fun to get it going and done.

How simple to be it done dumb.

How simple to be it done not dumb.

Simple to be it begun and done and re-done complex.

Complex to be it begun and done and re-done simple.

How done to know it beginning not done.

How undone to know it not done to begin.

And guy baldest ego rolled in to get it done gravely and won it.

And gal baldest ego rolled in to get it done sprightly and won it.

Raucous how fun to rip it apart soon.

Raucous how fun to rip it apart soon and slap.

Back.

Later.

Freighter.

Together.

Now that you know when you're done. Doing.

Now that you're doing what you didn't know. Begun.

And guy modest ego rolled in to get it done neo-baroquely post-modernist
and won it.

And gal modest ego rolled in to get it done neo-classically post-modernist
and won it.

Lift.

It'd help if there were a substantially heavy socially-accented sign right splat
in the middle of all this.

Cultural hydraulics.

Capital dynamics.

The winged-feet, flexing, remain ready.

Quo magis aeternum da dictis, diva, leporem.

"Therefore all the more grant to my speech, goddess, an ever-living charm."

Load.

And here goes all the way to ten or twenty or thirty or forty or fifty people.

And here fifty or forty or thirty or twenty people go some of the way of all
the way.

Curving around into the next sequence.

Curving around into the next sequence after that one this.

Minus the interloper equals a moment first.

A moment first add the interloper equals a moment second.

A moment second minus the interloper equals a moment third.

A moment third add the interloper equals a moment fourth.

The one.

Constitutive mainly the one.

The mark.

Unload.

Configuration re-sets.

How could that if ever that as that.

How does this if ever this as this.

How anyone not one as one.

Stacked.

The threshold mass-unit.

They see.

They hear.

Some asseverate.

All calculate.

Shipped out.

Soon or.

To "shape-up" comes from surplus amassment on the docks.

To be picked to labor.

To plabor be plicked.

Ecce.

The interloper.

Poetry-scene lurker as mass-popular unit.

Loner among.

Mass-popular unit as spark.

The one worth reading to.

You.

from *Kiosk* and *Rattapallax*

PAUL VIOLI

Appeal to the Grammarians

◊ ◊ ◊

We, the naturally hopeful,
Need a simple sign
For the myriad ways we're capsized.
We who love precise language
Need a finer way to convey
Disappointment and perplexity.
For speechlessness and all its inflections,
For up-ended expectations,
For every time we're ambushed
By trivial or stupefying irony,
For pure incredulity, we need
The inverted exclamation point.
For the dropped smile, the limp handshake,
For whoever has just unwrapped a dumb gift
Or taken the first sip of a flat beer,
Or felt love or pond ice
Give way underfoot, we deserve it.
We need it for the air pocket, the scratch shot,
The child whose ball doesn't bounce back,
The flat tire at journey's outset,
The odyssey that ends up in Weehawken.
But mainly because I need it—here and now
As I sit outside the Caffè Reggio
Staring at my espresso and cannoli
After this middle-aged couple
Came strolling by and he suddenly

Veered and sneezed all over my table
And she said to him, "See, *that's* why
I don't like to eat outside."

from *Green Mountains Review*

DAVID WAGONER

Trying to Make Music

◇　◇　◇

A poet is trying to make music
out of the tumult of the dictionary.
—Boris Pasternak

Getting the right words in the right order
    Is everyone's problem, but trying to make music
        At the same time (and often having to turn
And shut your mouth for a moment
    At the end of what you imagine is the end
        Of a line) is a poet's burden. All around you
And even inside your head the giggling and shouting
    Go on and on, the deliberate misquotations
        From someone you can't remember and don't want to,
And even if angels or that grizzly hag, your muse,
    Were to dictate directly, clearly *sotto voce*
        A perfect poem into your earhole,
The signature would seem wrong. The key would seem wrong.
    And along the mildewed corridors
        And high through the tiers of the echoing madhouse
You call your native tongue, you would hear
    The catcalls, the snide cackling, the whispering
        From cell to cell at the same time as the Voice
Of the loudspeaker is babbling something crucial
    And the chorus of tone-deaf guards is bellowing
        Lock-down and Body Search! Silence and Lights Out!

from *Hanging Loose*

In Praise of Han Shan

◊　◊　◊

Cold Mountain and Cold Mountain became the same thing in the mind,
The first last seen
        slipping into a crevice in the second.
Only the poems remained,
          scrawled on the rocks and trees,
Nothing's undoing among the self-stung unfolding of things.

from *Five Points*

CONTRIBUTORS'
NOTES AND
COMMENTS

KIM ADDONIZIO was born in Washington, D.C., in 1954 and now resides in Oakland, California. She is the author of four books of poetry: *The Philosopher's Club* (1994), *Jimmy & Rita* (1997), and *Tell Me* (2000), all from BOA Editions; and *What Is This Thing Called Love* (W. W. Norton, 2004). *Tell Me* was a finalist for the National Book Award. She has written a collection of stories, *In the Box Called Pleasure* (FC2, 1999). She is coauthor, with Dorianne Laux, of *The Poet's Companion: A Guide to the Pleasures of Writing Poetry* (W. W. Norton, 1997), and coeditor, with Cheryl Dumesnil, of *Dorothy Parker's Elbow: Tattoos on Writers, Writers on Tattoos* (Warner Books, 2002).

Of "Chicken," Addonizio writes: "Sometimes I look at jokes and riddles as a kind of poetry: alternate universes of compressed narratives and lyrics where one is in a state of uncertainty, mystery, and expectation. They're structured for surprise, the *aha!* of revelation or sudden laughter. Like the riddle of the lightbulb, the simple, familiar riddle of the chicken has generated its own literary tradition, responsive to cultural changes (Why did the punk rocker cross the road?) and further elaborations of meaning (Emerson: She didn't cross the road, she transcended it; Mark Twain: The news of its crossing has been greatly exaggerated). The original, ur-chicken riddle has such an obvious answer that the answer fails to satisfy. Instead, it propels us into a deeper consideration of existential realities and of our inherently conflicted relationship to poultry. *Why* did she want to get to the other side? Is there a goal, a destination, a place to go? What about free-range chickens? Maybe this little riddle is a secular koan which could free us from our cages, from the maya of materiality."

WILL ALEXANDER was born in South Central Los Angeles, California, in 1948. He graduated from UCLA and currently works for Beyond Baroque Press in Venice, California. His books include *Vertical Rainbow Climber* (Jazz Press, 1987), *Arcane Lavender Morals* (Leave Books, 1994), *Asia & Haiti* (Sun and Moon Press, 1995), *The Statospheric Canticles* (Pantograph Press, 1995), *Towards the Primeval Lightning Field* (O Books, 1998), *Above the Human Nerve Domain* (Pavement Saw Press, 1999), *Impulses & Nothingness* (Green Integer Books, 2004), and *The Sri Lankan Loxodrome* (Canopic Press, 2004). He notes, "A whole list of influences would be out of the question in this context, but let me mention in disparate order, Antonin Artaud, Aimé Césaire, Bob Kaufman, André Breton, Philip Lamantia, Ananda Coomaraswamy, and Sri Aurobindo. My poetic frequency combines the subconscious, conscious, and supraconscious minds. A trebled level working over and beyond itself, combining language inspired by African animism, shamanism, surrealism and its infinite conduits, infused with the incessant vertical motion of Aurobindo's 'Divine.'"

Of "Solea of the Simooms," Alexander writes: "Writing this work was like trying to transfix the elusive elementals of the mirage. I was attempting in 'Solea' to work with a language not unlike the inscrutable motion found in the symbols of jasper and blood. In another sense it is a song of cosmological isolation and wandering. But in the end, it is poetry which contains in its substance the power always hidden by invisibility."

BRUCE ANDREWS was born in Chicago, Illinois, on April Fool's Day, 1948. He is the author of *Lip Service* (Coach House Press, 2001), a recasting of Dante's *Paradiso. Jacket 22*, online at jacketmagazine.com, contains a symposium on this book. *The Millennium Project*, a thousand-page sequence, is online at Craig Dworkin's Eclipse site (eclipse.princeton.edu). Other titles include *Ex Why Zee* (Roof Books, 1995) and *Getting Ready to Have Been Frightened* (Roof Books, 1998). His essays on poetics are collected in *Paradise & Method: Poetics & Praxis* (Northwestern University Press, 1996). He is the former coeditor, with Charles Bernstein, of *L=A=N=G=U=A=G=E* (1978–1982) and *The L=A=N=G=U=A=G=E Book* (Southern Illinois University Press, 1984). Andrews has taught political science at Fordham University since 1975.

Andrews writes: "'Dang Me' is a recent prose sequence dedicated to the newer discombobulating poetic work of one of my favorite younger authors — Kevin Davies (from Brooklyn via Vancouver)."

RAE ARMANTROUT was born in Vallejo, California, in 1947. Her most recent books are *Up to Speed* (Wesleyan University Press, 2004), *Veil: New and Selected Poems* (Wesleyan University Press, 2001), and *The Pretext* (Green Integer Books, 2001). She lives in San Diego and teaches at the University of California, San Diego.

Armantrout writes: "It's hard to decide what to say about 'Almost.' It's a poem in two sections, each dealing with the relation of language to the self. Each begins pretty reasonably and becomes less sensible as it proceeds. The last three lines may (or may not) gesture toward 'the lyric.'"

CRAIG ARNOLD was born in Merced, California, in 1967. His first book, *Shells* (Yale University Press, 1999), was the 1998 winner of the Yale Younger Poets Competition. His performances have been featured at Chicago's Uptown Poetry Slam, South by Southwest Music and Media Conference in Austin, Texas, and the KGB Bar Monday Night Poetry series in New York. He has been a Hodder Fellow in the Humanities at Princeton, and has taught at the University of South Dakota.

Of "Your friend's arriving on the bus," Arnold writes: "The poem happened in Granada, which was the last part of Arab Andalucía to capitulate to the Christian invasion in 1492. One may visit its wonderful Moorish palaces and gardens, including the Alhambra, and in the older quarter of town, the Albaicín, there are many teahouses where one may sit and play chess and drink very hot, very sweet mint tea. It was also the hometown of the great poet Federico García Lorca, but he doesn't really come into this poem at all. Neither do the Moors, the palaces, or the mint tea, but I mention them because I don't want people to think I had only an unpleasant time there. My friend was coming on the bus from, I think, Paris. Her name is Sandrine."

JOHN ASHBERY was born in Rochester, New York, in 1927. He is the author of more than twenty books of poetry, including *Chinese Whispers* (2002), *Your Name Here* (2000), *Girls on the Run* (1999), and *Wakefulness* (1998), all from Farrar, Straus and Giroux. His *Self-Portrait in a Convex Mirror* received the Pulitzer Prize, the National Book Critics Circle Award, and the National Book Award. He is currently the Charles P. Stevenson, Jr., Professor of Languages and Literature at Bard College. He was the guest editor of *The Best American Poetry 1988*.

MARY JO BANG was born in Waynesville, Missouri, in 1946, and grew up in St. Louis. Educated at Northwestern University, the Polytechnic of Central London, and Columbia University, she is the author of *Apology for Want* (University Press of New England, 1997), *Louise in Love* (Grove Press, 2001), and *The Downstream Extremity of the Isle of Swans* (University of Georgia Press, 2001). Her fourth book of poems, *The Eye Like a Strange Balloon*, will be published by Grove Press in 2004. She has been a poetry editor at *Boston Review* since 1995. She teaches at Washington University in St. Louis.

Of "The Eye Like a Strange Balloon Mounts Toward Infinity," Bang writes: "The title is the same as that of a charcoal sketch by Odilon Redon (later used as a lithograph for a book of Poe translations, *A Edgar Poe*). The image is dark, arresting, perplexing, and (depending upon one's sense of humor) amusing. Freudian before Freud, surreal before Breton, at the center of an empty rectangle of roughed-in sky, a hot-air balloon in the form of an eyeball floats above an ill-defined horizon that might be a desolate landscape or a body of water (either way, a vague sense of threat, strong sense of solitude). The pupil is positioned up, so it sees everything it's headed for. Strings attach a basket so shallow it looks like a tray; on that quasi-tray is the top half of a head with two slightly sad (quite possibly horrified) eyes looking forward. Poor head, it has no say in where it's being taken. At the apex of the eye-balloon, side to side, there's a fine coxcomb of lash, indicating the presumed presence of an eyelid. The balloon continues to take in what it sees, all against the threat of a sight-obliterating blink."

ALAN BERNHEIMER was born in New York City in 1948 and has lived in the San Francisco Bay Area since the mid-1970s. His most recent collection of poems is *Billionesque* (The Figures, 1999). *Cloud Eight* (Sound & Language, 1999) collected his collaborations with Kit Robinson. Earlier books include *Café Isotope* (The Figures, 1980) and *State Lounge* (Tuumba Press, 1981).

Of "20 Questions," Bernheimer writes: "The first question came to me in the wake of the terrorist attacks of September 11, 2001. I had heard the United States Poet Laureate on the radio say that poetry was too personal to respond directly to the enormity of the events. That didn't sound adequate. Soon I realized there were a good number of other questions for which I did not have an answer, a good number like twenty, and it would be interesting to orchestrate the play of these questions against one another to see how they responded."

CHARLES BERNSTEIN was born in Manhattan in 1950. His published collections of poetry include *With Strings* (University of Chicago Press, 2001), *Republics of*

Reality: Poems 1975–1995 (Sun and Moon Press, 2000), *Controlling Interests* (1980; rpt., Roof Books, 2004), and *The Sophist* (1987; rpt., Salt Books, 2004). His essays are found in *My Way: Speeches and Poems* (University of Chicago Press, 1999) and *Content's Dream: Essays, 1975–1984* (1986; rpt., Northwestern University Press, 2001). He edited *Close Listening: Poetry and the Performed Word* (Oxford University Press, 1998) and *99 Poets/1999: An International Poetics Symposium* (Duke University Press, 1998). He teaches at the University of Pennsylvania.

Of "Sign Under Test," Bernstein writes: "If culture were an accident, then the job of the poet might be to write the report rather than rectify the wrong. If culture were the product of a supreme fiction, then the poet's job might be to find the authors and clue them in to things—not as they are but as they appear.

"Everyone is talking about memoir but I just want to forget. I want a poetry that helps me to forget what I never knew.

"I embrace a poetics of bewilderment. I don't know where I am going and never have, just try to grapple as best I can with where I am. The poetry that most engages me is not theoretically perspicacious, indeed it has a poetics and an aesthetics but not a predetermining theory; it is multiform and chaotic, always reformulating and regrouping. Competence is less important to me than responsiveness; mobility; ingenuity and invention more important than solutions to predefined problems.

"I don't want to make poems that tell you what to think but that show a different order of thinking."

ANSELM BERRIGAN was born in Chicago, Illinois, in 1972. He grew up in New York City and lives there now after spending time in Buffalo and San Francisco. His books include *Zero Star Hotel* (2002) and *Integrity and Dramatic Life* (1999), both from Edge Books. Other titles include *Strangers in the Nest, They Beat Me Over the Head with a Sack,* and *In the Dream Hole* (with his brother, Edmund Berrigan). He is the artistic director of the Poetry Project at St. Mark's Church in the Bowery in New York City.

Of "Token Enabler," Berrigan writes: "This poem was written during the spring of 2002. It was an attempt to use a long, uninterrupted line in an effort to include language from as many sources as I could. The language of cable television news covering the War on Terrorism came into play, as did the fact of having to inject our bird (named Pig) with psychotropic drugs prescribed by a vet to deal with his high anxiety due to construction in our building—it was causing him to yank out his own feathers. On some basic level, the poem is concerned with handling fear; that of a semi-paranoid public, and that of a little birdy being forced to take a human concoction."

MARK BIBBINS was born in Albany, New York, in 1968. His first book of poems, *Sky Lounge* (Graywolf Press, 2003), was a Lambda Book Award finalist. He has taught at the New School, where he cofounded *LIT* magazine, and at Purchase College. He lives in Manhattan.

Bibbins writes: "'Blasted Fields of Clover Bring Harrowing and Regretful Sighs' is a poem in seventeen sections of roughly the same length. The thing concerns itself primarily with saturation, velocity, and sex as it might be had by machines. Its trigger was 'Rae,' the third track on Autechre's 'LP5' (Warp

Records, 1998). Two years after writing the poem, I constructed for it an aural footnote called 'Clover,' which can be accessed via www.markbibbins.com."

ONI BUCHANAN was born in Hershey, Pennsylvania, in 1975. She completed her undergraduate degrees in English and music at the University of Virginia, then attended the Iowa Writers' Workshop for an MFA degree in poetry. In May 2004, she completed a master's degree in music (piano performance) at the New England Conservatory of Music. Her first book of poetry, *What Animal*, appeared from the University of Georgia Press in October 2003. She lives in Boston.

Buchanan writes: "'The Walk' is a waking nightmare kind of poem in which the protagonist continually must reevaluate the type of imminent danger which confronts her, because the protean woman in the woods continuously changes her guises and her implements of violence as she approaches. The rapping of the cloth-covered brick and the rasp of the woman's voice counting send the landscape into a rocketing of expansions and contractions, a telescoping of both the physical dimensions of the landscape as well as its temporal existence. This drastic shift in perspective serves (among other things) to populate the previously deserted landscape with hypothetical dwellers and their noises, their occupations, their means of survival."

MICHAEL BURKARD was born in Rome, New York, in 1947. He is the author of *In a White Light* (L'Epervier Press, 1977), *Ruby for Grief* (University of Pittsburgh Press, 1981), *The Fires They Kept* (Metro Book Co., 1986), *Fictions from the Self* (W. W. Norton, 1987), *My Secret Boat: A Notebook of Prose and Poems* (W. W. Norton, 1990), *Entire Dilemma* (Sarabande Books, 1998), *Unsleeping* (Sarabande Books, 2001) and *Pennsylvania Collection Agency* (New Issues Press, 2001). He teaches in the graduate writing program at Syracuse University.

Of "a cloud of dusk," Burkard writes: "The poem is part of a series of poems I wrote two years ago, and then began taking out of sequence. Now the series is intact again."

ANNE CARSON was born in Canada in 1950 and teaches ancient Greek for a living. Her recent books, all from Knopf, include *Autobiography of Red* (1998), *Men in the Off Hours* (2000), *The Beauty of the Husband* (2001), and a translation of the fragments of Sappho entitled *If Not, Winter* (2002).

Of "Gnosticism," Carson writes: "A gnostic is someone who is walking along lost in the dark and hears a cry. So I walk."

T. J. CLARK was born in Bristol, England, in 1943. He has lived in the United States for the past twenty-five years, teaching art history for a living—for the past fifteen years at the University of California, Berkeley. Most of his published work centers on nineteenth- and twentieth-century painting, especially in France. *The Absolute Bourgeois: Artists and Politics in France, 1848–1851*, first published in 1973, appeared in a new paperback edition from the University of California Press in 1999. His other books include *Image of the People: Gustave Courbet and the 1848 Revolution* (1973; paperback ed., University of California Press, 1999) and *The Painting of Modern Life: Paris in the Art of Manet and his Followers* (1984; paperback ed., Princeton University Press, 1999). *Farewell to an Idea: Episodes from a History of Modernism* was published by Yale University Press in 1999.

Of "Landscape with a Calm," Clark writes: "This is the first poem I've published in forty years. It came out of an opportunity I had a couple of years ago to look repeatedly, morning after morning, at two paintings by Poussin, 'Landscape with a Calm' and 'Landscape with a Man Killed by a Snake.' This and other poems occurred, unexpectedly, as part of a series of diary entries I made, trying to keep track of the ways the paintings changed as I went back to them, and reflecting on what it was in the paintings that seemed to compel (and reward) the looking again."

BILLY COLLINS was born in the French Hospital in New York City in 1941. His books of poetry include *Nine Horses* (Random House, 2002), *Sailing Alone Around the Room: New and Selected Poems* (Random House, 2001), *Picnic, Lightning* (University of Pittsburgh Press, 1998), *The Art of Drowning* (University of Pittsburgh Press, 1995), and *Questions About Angels* (William Morrow, 1991), which was selected for the National Poetry Series by Edward Hirsch and reprinted by the University of Pittsburgh Press in 1999. He edited *Poetry 180: A Turning Back to Poetry* (Random House, 2003). He teaches at Lehman College (City University of New York). This is his ninth appearance in *The Best American Poetry*. He served as United States Poet Laureate from 2001 to 2003.

Of "The Centrifuge," Collins writes: "I wrote this poem after a couple of months of near zero production. The poet laureate road show, as I had been warned, had taken me far from my own writing, and I remember at the time feeling glad to be writing anything other than my name on the inside of a book. I took it as a good sign that I did not understand this poem. I still do not know who that family is, and I haven't a clue as to what's in that suitcase. Nothing is my best guess.

"With the advantage of hindsight, I can see now that the poem draws on two unrelated sources. The first is the Great Exhibition of 1900 in Paris, the inspiration for Henry Adams's essay 'The Virgin and the Dynamo,' in which Adams claims a religious power for the new technology represented at the fair by a hall of dynamos—my centrifuge. The second is the early films of Hitchcock, made in England, especially the one with the spookiest title, 'The Lodger.' Of course, none of the above should be understood as a ticket of admission to the poem."

JACK COLLOM was born in Chicago, Illinois, in 1931. He makes a living teaching poetry to small children and to college students at Naropa University. In 2001 Tuumba Press published a selected volume of his poems, *Red Car Goes By*.

Of "3-4-00," Collom writes, "I was surprised at first that it was chosen to be published at all, but repeated readings convince me it's a happy little marriage (dance) of fact and a bit of mindflow."

MICHAEL COSTELLO was born in Buffalo, New York, in 1976. He received his BA from SUNY Fredonia and holds an MFA degree from New School University. He lives in Albany, New York, and works as an editor for Palio Communications, in Saratoga Springs.

Of "Ode to My Flint and Boom Bolivia," Costello writes: "It began as an ode to my flesh-and-blood body. I had recently read Pablo Neruda's odes, and thought I would try to write one. I enjoyed writing in the celebratory tone of the ode form, but I found myself feeling static about the content. I am process-oriented and have become familiar with the writings of the Oulipo. My experiments have led me to combine free-form writing with various types of processes in the manner of Ted Berrigan's *Sonnets*. I find that by putting my writing through a preconceived process, I can create a tension or energy. The process I applied here turned the poem inside out. It suddenly became an ode to the external world (everything outside of my body) as opposed to being the ode to my body (everything internal). I was very excited with the result."

MICHAEL DAVIDSON was born in Oakland, California, in 1944. He teaches literature at the University of California, San Diego. He is the author of *Guys Like Us: Citing Masculinity in Cold War Poetics* (University Chicago Press, 2003), *Ghostlier Demarcations: Modern Poetry and the Material Word* (University of California Press, 1997), and *The San Francisco Renaissance: Poetics and Community at Mid-Century* (Cambridge University Press, 1989). He has written eight collections of poems, including *The Arcades* (O Books, 1998), *Post Hoc* (Avenue B, 1990), and *The Landing of Rochambeau* (Burning Deck, 1985).

Davidson writes: "'Bad Modernism' is part of a suite of poems that attempts to deal with more problematic or embarrassing aspects of modernism—its will to power, its racism, its imperialism—from within particular 'voices' created within modernism. In this version, 'Bad Modernism,' tries to imagine a streamlined corporate space in which all aspects of knowledge and agency can be found in separate suites on different floors, in which thought itself appears as a kind of office party for patrons who are filled with loathing, yet who are 'seeking interpretation.'"

OLENA KALYTIAK DAVIS was born in Detroit in 1963. She is the author of two books of poetry, *shattered sonnets love cards and other off and back handed importunities* (Tin House/Bloomsbury, 2003) and *And Her Soul Out of Nothing* (University of Wisconsin, 1997). She is the mother of two children, Avgustyn and Olyana. She lives in Anchorage, Alaska.

Of "You Art A Scholar, Horatio, Speak To It," Kalytiak Davis writes: "According to the evidence in my commonplace book of the time (September, 1998), I had recently reread *Hamlet*, but was most immediately responding to this tripartite (unattributed in my tablet) description: 'brow-hanging, shoe-contemplative, strange.' The thought was to make the seemingly and semi-educated-literateandry-detached part of myself try to understand, reason with, and perhaps even exorcise, the undying döppelganger of my unreasonable, obsessive, and totally unrequited (?!?!) feelings for/about, let's call them/it, X. Or at least attribute some adjectives to it. To descry by describing and describe by decrying, or so the notes say. Turns out no part of me wasn't complicit, was up for/to it."

JEAN DAY was born in Syracuse, New York, in 1954, and grew up in Rhode Island. In the mid-1970s she moved to the San Francisco Bay Area, where she has worked as a house painter and amanuensis, a book packer, acquisitions manager, and then director of Small Press Distribution; and as an editor and writer. She is currently managing editor of *Representations*, an interdisciplinary humanities journal published by the University of California Press. She is the author of six books of poetry, among them *Enthusiasm: Odes & Otium* (forthcoming), *The Literal World* (Atelos, 1998), and *The I and the You* (Potes & Poets, 1992). Her work has also appeared in several anthologies, including *Moving Borders: Three Decades of Innovative Writing by Women* (Talisman House, 1998).

Day writes: "'Prose of the World Order' is an ode from *Enthusiasm*. I had written a book (*The Literal World*) full of American cranks and idealists and found myself still in their grip. Odes (or, more likely, an 'odic poetics') seemed to me to offer a kind of lyric overdrive beginning in sheer personality and ending (Whitman-like) in its populist enthusiastic overflow. Some of the obvious plunderings in the poem (Merleau-Ponty's famously borrowed title; Beckett's riff from *Molloy*) refer to the play between plainness and grandiosity that make the institution of the human so ridiculous and so compelling."

LINH DINH was born in Saigon in 1963 and came to the United States in 1975. In recent years he has also lived in Italy. He is the author of two collections of stories, *Blood and Soap* (Seven Stories Press, 2004) and *Fake House* (Seven Stories Press, 2000), and a book of poems, *All Around What Empties Out* (Tinfish, 2003). His work has been anthologized in *The Best American Poetry 2000* and *Great American Prose Poems: From Poe to the Present* (Scribner, 2003). He edited the anthologies *Night, Again: Contemporary Fiction from Vietnam* (Seven Stories Press, 1996) and *Three Vietnamese Poets* (Tinfish, 2001).

Of "13," Dinh writes: "I've always been a reader of trash literature. The worse the writing, the more I love it. I get off on flawed thinking expressed in bad English. This poem was inspired by horoscopes. The poet as an oracle as a fortune-teller. I love the authoritative voice in horoscopes. Since fortune-tellers already know the future, the present and the past are nothing to them. They also know exactly who you are. During a long cab ride in Singapore, the driver told me exactly who I was, down to the last detail. He had nearly everything wrong, of course, but I loved his attitude. The man was charming and foolish enough to be a poet."

RITA DOVE was born in Akron, Ohio, in 1952. Her poetry collections include the forthcoming *American Smooth* (W. W. Norton), *On the Bus with Rosa Parks* (W. W. Norton, 1999), *Mother Love* (W. W. Norton, 1995), *Selected Poems* (Pantheon/Vintage, 1993), *Grace Notes* (W. W. Norton, 1989), and *Thomas and Beulah* (Carnegie-Mellon University, 1986). She is also the author of a book of short stories, *Fifth Sunday* (Callaloo Fiction Series) (University of Virginia, 1985), a novel, *Through the Ivory Gate* (Pantheon, 1992), a volume of essays, *The Poet's World* (Library of Congress, 1995), and a play, *The Darker Face of the Earth* (Story Line Press, 2000), which had its world premiere in 1996 at the Oregon Shakespeare Festival and was subsequently produced at the Kennedy Center in Washington, D.C., and the Royal National Theatre in London. *Seven for Luck*, a song cycle for soprano and orchestra with music by John Williams, was premiered by the Boston Symphony in 1998, and she collaborated with John Williams on Steven Spielberg's Millennium documentary *The Unfinished Journey*. In 1987 she received the Pulitzer Prize in poetry. She served as Poet Laureate of the United States from 1993 to 1995 and as special consultant for the Library of Congress bicentennial in 1999–2000. She is Commonwealth Professor of

English at the University of Virginia in Charlottesville. She was the guest editor of *The Best American Poetry 2000*.

Of "All Souls'," Dove writes: "Our house burned down after a lightning strike in 1998. During the subsequent rebuilding and refurnishing, I didn't have much inclination to write at all; it took about six months before the poems began to reappear—shy, erratic blossoms poking their heads up through the ashes—and always without warning or, as far as I could tell, logic. The beginnings of 'All Souls" arose at this time, the first scribbled entry in a brand-new notebook. I liked what was there—the cadences and authorial distance—but I didn't yet understand its urgency, its raison d'être, so I put the draft away in a drawer. Then came 9/11, and somehow its haunting images of catastrophe sent me back to those abandoned lines. Endings, beginnings; to linger in regret or to move on: I found myself turning back to the front of that notebook, reconsidering what had been jotted down years before, in haste and incomprehension . . . and I finished the poem."

RACHEL BLAU DUPLESSIS was born in Brooklyn, New York, in 1941, and lives in Philadelphia, where she teaches at Temple University. Her first book of poetry appeared in 1980 and her long poem project, begun in 1986, has been collected so far in *Draft, unnumbered: Précis* (Nomados, 2003) and *Drafts 1–38, Toll* (Wesleyan University Press, 2001). She edited *The Selected Letters of George Oppen* (Duke University Press, 1990). Her literary criticism may be found in *Genders, Races, and Religious Cultures in Modern American Poetry, 1908–1934* (Cambridge University Press, 2001).

DuPlessis writes: "'Draft 55: Quiptych' (a made-up word parallel to triptych) is a poem in quatrains headed up by a citation from Herakleitos about randomness as an organizing principle; it also takes hold of a remark by Gertrude Stein concerning two things—the dictionary and the country. The poem is dedicated to the scholar-critic Peter Quartermain, and it puns a lot on '4' since this number is imbedded in his name. Poems in the book manuscript from which 'Quiptych' comes (*Drafts 39–57, Pledge*) are all dedicated to individuals, and all had to obey, loosely, the rule of citation or allusion to prior poems in their 'line' on the grid pattern that I use to organize my long poem project. By using the general title *Drafts*, I signal that all these poems are open to transformation, part of an ongoing process of construction, self-commentary, textual examination, and reconstruction. This has parallels with the genre called 'midrash' in Hebrew textuality. A lot of the poems I am writing seem to cross between essay (in argument), story (in length), and poem (in heft and mechanism). The poems in this book manuscript were also deeply marked by the political events both preceding and following the crisis of 9/11. In 'Draft 55: Quiptych,' there is a description of papermaking, a general description of the endless, somewhat random process of making something by combining other things (that is, a description of art itself), and the presentation of a four-folded, imaginary mini-altar, the quiptych, that turns out to be the poem itself."

kari edwards, who was born in Rantoul, Illinois, in 1954, prefers the use of "sie" as a gender-neutral pronoun and favors lowercase letters. edwards is a poet, artist, and gender activist; winner of a New Langton Arts Bay Area Award in literature (2002); author of *iduna* (O Books, 2003), *a day in the life of p.* (subpress collective, 2002), *a diary of lies—Belladonna #27* (Belladonna Books, 2002), *obLiqUE paRt(itON): colLABorationS* (xPress(ed), 2002), and *post/(pink)* (Scarlet Press, 2000). edwards is also the poetry editor of I.F.G.E's *Transgender Tapestry*, an international publication on transgender issues.

Of "short sorry," edwards writes: "as if all points in the positional grind brought their own narrative to describe one's life; 'short sorry' is as if the auto-biographical rhizome of everything in one's life is/was caramelized to a non-narrative narrative, neither nor or not, a poem or story or narrative or not-not."

KENWARD ELMSLIE was born in New York City in 1929. His publications include the Frank O'Hara Award–winning *Motor Disturbance* (Columbia University Press, 1971), *Bare Bones* (Bamberger Books, 1995), *Routine Disruptions: Selected Poems & Lyrics, 1960–1998* (Coffee House Press, 1998), *Cyberspace* (Granary Books, 2000), *Blast from the Past* (Skanky Possum, 2000), and *Agenda Melt* (Adventures in Poetry). In April 2004, a musical review, *Lingo Land*—a retrospective culled from his six opera librettos, five musical plays, and innumerable poem songs—was produced off-Broadway by the York Theatre. Elmslie spends winters in New York City and summers in Calais, Vermont.

Elmslie writes: "'Sibling Rivalry' conjoins earthbound memories of my Colorado Springs boyhood (overt narrative) and fragmented stanzas, narrative present and hopefully accounted for, but layered within a shifting vortex of past, present, and fantasy-ridden imaginings of a future."

AARON FOGEL was born in New York in 1947. His books include *The Printer's Error* (poems; Miami University Press, 2001), *Coercion to Speak: Conrad's Poetics of Dialogue* (Harvard University Press, 1985), and *Chain Hearings* (poems; Inwood/Horizon Press, 1976). He teaches at Boston University. His work appeared in the 1989, 1990, and 1995 editions of *The Best American Poetry* and in the anthology *Ecstatic Occasions, Expedient Forms* (Michigan, 1995).

Of "370,000, December, 2000," Fogel writes: "Alfreda Murck's *Poetry and Painting in Song China: The Subtle Art of Dissent* was the source for some of this poem's images and for the line about 'Refining cinnabar.' '337,000' was a number in the news in December 2000, but can also be seen as a picture. Parts of the poem were written carefully, parts were done almost by automatic writing. When it appeared in *Pataphysics*, there was no author's name attached to it on the page. I like that anonymity and wish in some way it could remain unsigned."

ARIELLE GREENBERG was born in Columbus, Ohio, in 1972 and grew up in Schenectady, New York. She received a BA from Purchase College, a public arts school, then worked for cultural nonprofits in New York City before completing an MFA from Syracuse University. She is the author of *Given* (Verse Press, 2002) and coeditor, with Rachel Zucker, of an anthology of essays by young women poets writing about influences upon them (forthcoming from Wesleyan University Press in 2005). She teaches in the poetry program at Columbia College in Chicago.

Of "Saints," Greenberg writes: "As a child I loved that my first name—in its original spelling, Ariel (changed when my family lived in Israel for a year to indicate that I was a girl)—was on the cover of a slim volume my mother kept with the Bibles and art books in our house. I started writing poetry at a very young age, so for a long time, Plath was my lodestar, and everything I wrote dark and cynical. Finally, in grad school, I realized that many of the writers I loved most were the playful ones (Joyce, Nabokov, McHugh, Tate, Notley), and I made a conscious effort to welcome humor and joy into my work. My mentor, Michael Burkard, encouraged me to move in this direction, a direction that still seems risky, if one takes the humor seriously (and I do). I also draw inspiration from other women artists of my generation who dare to make serious art with the cute, the ephemeral, and the girly (I've coined a term for this, The Gurlesque, and written about it—there's some online). 'Saints' illustrates these risks, and therefore alarms me slightly: I'm represented by a poem about a grilled cheese sandwich! I wrote the poem because I was amused by the phrase/rhyme 'chives of the saints.' The stuff about the waitress is based on a real waitress who spoke with spontaneous, genuine kindness, and kindness in everyday encounters seems a blessing to me. And as a Jew, I've always had saint envy."

TED GREENWALD was born in Brooklyn, New York, in 1942. His most recent books are *The Up and Up* (Atelos, 2004) and *Jumping the Line* (Roof Books, 1998).

BARBARA GUEST was born in Wilmington, North Carolina, in 1920. She graduated from the University of California at Berkeley, went to New York City, and is connected to the New York School of Poets. She has received the Poetry Society of America's Robert Frost Medal. She has published twenty-three books of poetry, including *Symbiosis* (Kelsey St. Press, 2000), *If So, Tell Me* (Reality Street Editions, 1999), and *Rocks on a Platter: Notes on Literature* (Wesleyan University Press, 1999). In 2003 appeared a reprint of her biography of H. D. (Hilda Doolittle), *Herself Defined: The Poet H. D. and Her World* (Schaffner Press) and *Miniatures and Other Poems* (Wesleyan University Press). Also appearing in 2003 were a book of essays on poetics, *Forces of Imagination: Writing on Writing* (Kelsey St. Press), and *Dürer in the Window* (Roof Books), a book of essays, reviews, and poems on art.

Guest writes: "'Nostalgia of the Infinite' is the beginning of my exploration into Surrealist poems. The paintings of the Surrealist Giorgio de Chirico were my first introduction to Surrealism. This was followed by a series of Surrealist poems, included now in my book *The Red Gaze. Surrealism and Other Poems* (Wesleyan University Press, 2005)."

CARLA HARRYMAN was born in Orange, California, in 1952. Her books include *Gardener of Stars* (Atelos Press, 2001), *The Words: After Carl Sandburg's Rootabaga Stories and Jean-Paul Sartre* (Tuumba Press, 1999), *There Never Was a Rose Without a Thorn* (City Lights Books, 1995), *Memory Play* (O Books, 1994), *In the Mode Of* (Zasterle Press, 1991), *Animal Instincts* (Sun and Moon Press, 1989), *Vice* (Potes & Poets Press, 1986), *The Middle* (Gaz, 1984), *Property* (Tuumba Press, 1981), *Under the Bridge* (This Press, 1980), and *Percentage* (Tuumba Press, 1979). The complete *Baby* is forthcoming from Adventures in Poetry in Spring 2005. She is on the faculty of Wayne State University in Detroit.

JANE HIRSHFIELD was born in New York City in 1953 and has lived in the San Francisco Bay Area since 1974. Her most recent poetry collection, *Given Sugar, Given Salt* (HarperCollins, 2001), was a finalist for the National Book Critics

Circle Award and winner of the Bay Area Book Reviewers Award. Other poetry books include *The Lives of the Heart* (HarperCollins, 1997), *The October Palace* (HarperCollins, 1994), *Of Gravity & Angels* (Wesleyan University Press, 1988), and *Alaya* (QRL Series, 1982). She has also published a collection of essays, *Nine Gates: Entering the Mind of Poetry* (HarperCollins, 1997), and two anthologies collecting the work of women poets from the past. She has taught in the Bennington College MFA Writing Program and at the University of California, Berkeley.

Of "Poe: An Assay (I)," Hirshfield writes: "This poem was the first of a series of poetic investigations I think of as 'assays.' The term, used in chemistry and in the mining industry, refers to the analysis of a substance to determine its component parts and their relative quantities. It's also of course related to 'essay,' and the assay-poems feel to me musical and conceptual hybrids, living somewhere between poetry and prose. They want to explore their subjects both plainly and obliquely, if that is possible; to take a thing apart by shining a light through it, and through our ideas of what it might be. I had reread Poe—the stories and critical writings—about a year before writing this poem, for an essay on the subject of hiddenness. It seems that Poe, whose genius I had in childhood found profoundly disturbing, had secreted himself under the floorboards of my own consciousness. In the fall of 2002, I found myself at Yaddo (the artists' colony in upstate New York, on whose grounds—long before it became an artists' colony—legend has it Poe wrote 'The Raven'), and this poem came forward. I think it was in part for me what Poe's stories, at least in my speculation, were for him: a way to engage with the horror of an increasingly darkening time. For my poem also has its omissions, something it points toward by naming his. The reader might pause to ask, 'What is it that goes similarly unspoken now, here? What is it we can't bear to see, but also cannot ignore?' This is one of the more mysterious strategies of art in facing what cannot be faced. The real work may be done off to the side, while the hands—like a magician's—are always seemingly in plain view. And that, and not the trick's ostensible outcome, is the point."

JOHN HOLLANDER was born in New York City in 1929. He has published eighteen books of poetry, the most recent being *Picture Window* (Knopf, 2003) and a reissue of his *Reflections on Espionage* with added notes and commentary (Yale University Press, 1999). His books of criticism include *The Work of Poetry* (Columbia University Press, 1999) and *The Poetry of Everyday Life* (University of Michigan Press, 1998). A MacArthur Fellow, he lives in Connecticut and is Sterling Professor Emeritus of English at Yale University. He was the guest editor of *The Best American Poetry 1998*.

Of "For 'Fiddle-De-Dee,'" Hollander writes: "This little jingle was scribbled as a sort of penance for a curmudgeonly refusal to acknowledge a bit of poetic license for too long. The exchange (in *Through the Looking-Glass*) between Alice and the Red Queen, quoted in my epigraph, goes on a bit further:

> Alice thought she saw a way out of the difficulty, this time. "If you'll tell me what language 'fiddle-de-dee' is, I'll tell you the French for it!" she exclaimed triumphantly.
> But the Red Queen drew herself up rather stiffly and said, "Queens never make bargains."

After being delighted by this in early childhood, I came to grow cross with the notion that 'fiddle-de-dee' wasn't English: it was nothing *but* English, not just the 'fiddle' but the 'de' and the 'dee' as well. These are all English, as, say, *'Stuss!'* (as my mother would say in my childhood) was German, for the same 'Nonsense!' (or, in the analogous higher diction in German, *'Unsinn!'*) No, 'fiddle-de-dee' *was* English and Alice was wrong; by not pointing this out, the Red Queen was, particularly for so authoritarian a personage, rather negligent. Later on, after having become a teacher myself, I got to be seriously interested in nonsense as one of poetry's congenially disruptive siblings, like dreaming, lying, chanting spells, and the others. I had even written a bit of commentary on the passage at one point. One day last year, the cadence of the Red Queen's question sounded in my ear again as it first had for me as a child (**'fid**dle-de-**dee'**), and in some kind of acknowledgment of Alice's assertion, I felt myself asking 'Well, in that case, what's the A for X, the B for Y,' etc., and the verses in question unrolled themselves. Queens may not make bargains, but poetry often does.

> But now let's change our point of view:
> What's the English for *turlututu*?
> It's "fiddle-de-dee" (I thought you knew)

FANNY HOWE was born in Buffalo, New York, in 1940, and grew up in Boston. She has recently taught at the University of California at San Diego and at New School University. Her most recent collections of poems are *Gone* (2003) and *Selected Poems* (2000), both from the University of California Press. Graywolf Press is publishing another collection, *On the Ground*, in 2004.

Howe writes: "'Catholic' is an effort at understanding Aquinas in contemporary terms, something that leads me in many directions, most of them surprising."

KENNETH IRBY was born in Bowie, Texas, in 1936, and is a graduate of the University of Kansas, Harvard University, and the University of California, Berkeley. He has lived, worked, served in the army, and taught in New Mexico, Nevada, the North Pacific, Massachusetts, New York, Colorado, and Copenhagen. His recent books include *In Denmark* (in the second issue of *No: a journal of the arts*, 2003), *Studies* (First Intensity Press, 2001), and *Ridge to Ridge* (OtherWind Press, 2001). He lives in Lawrence, Kansas, and teaches in the Department of English at the University of Kansas.

Of "[Record]," Irby writes: "It was written on a St. Patrick's Day afternoon, the crossings of the Saint, and the medieval poem once ascribed to him, and the presence of Ed Dorn, who comes back and comes back since his death, and the moment of the day and place itself. One friend said he would after all rather spend time with his grandchildren than consider such matters too closely, but the piece has always felt completely to be about that interaction. What is the exchange? As conversion or events or people or signs? And if not people, why not people? And if, what? The back and forth ('this door swings both ways'). So much so, it's always seemed the title was in fact 'Return.'"

MAJOR JACKSON was born in Philadelphia in 1968. His first book of poems, *Leaving Saturn*, published by the University of Georgia Press, was the recipient of the 2000 Cave Canem Poetry Prize and a finalist for the 2002 National Book Critics Circle Award. He is an assistant professor of English at the University of Vermont. His second book of poems, *Hoops*, is forthcoming from W. W. Norton in 2005.

Of "Urban Renewal," Jackson writes: "For all of my life, I have been asked if I am (or when I was younger was my father) a member of the military. In my family tree, 'Major' appears thrice, dating back four generations to pre–Civil War times. To some extent, the poem pays homage to the long and great naming practices of African-Americans, whereby enterprising parents sought to endow their children with enchanting names that when uttered evoked power, prestige, and glory, despite their lack of physical or economic empowerment.

"The battle for respect is continual for black people in America. Of late, I have been appalled by the derisive response to names that are plainly 'ethnic' in sound. Against this tide of mockery, I wanted to write about the strength in such names as Kareem, Amari, and Mustafa. Then, like a drowned corpse, an early memory surfaced of a substitute teacher assigned to my class for the week who called out the roll on the first day with extreme difficulty and wonder and returned the following day with new names for all of us. Although it was cloaked as part of her curriculum for the week, I recognized even then the arrogance and disrespect behind that kind of erasure. The revulsion, so representative of the average American toward their immigrant and native-born brothers and sisters, lay on her tongue. But these considerations fall short of the pleasures of composition. Normally, composing a poem is an exercise in failed play which makes the process fun. This was the first time I experienced a palpable pain in my gut as I was writing the poem through various drafts. I am normally not in favor of the didactic in poetry, but I am growing older and the urgency to change the world around me seems starker."

MARC JAFFEE was born in Memphis, Tennessee, in 1984. He lives in New York City and is currently attending Vassar College.

Of "King of Repetition," Jaffee writes: "I have almost no recollection of writing this poem. At the time, I was under the influence of Camus's *The Stranger*, which, for me, made powerlessness seem sexy. However, I feel that this poem is less a product of the existential 'absurd' than a collection of sensations I experienced as the gears of my disappearing childhood shifted into the cogs of my near-future. I was in my senior year of high school when I wrote it and I remember feeling the distinct sharpness of a change that becomes more perceptible with increased objectivity. I wanted to make myself, like Wallace Stevens's jar, both the subject of the poetic reality, and an object revealed in relation to other objects. The poem tumbled out of me like some adventurous baby. Once written down, the words sprang to life and asserted their own independence."

KENNETH KOCH was born in Cincinnati, Ohio, in 1925. After serving in the United States Army in World War II, seeing action as a rifleman in the Philippines, he went to Harvard on the GI Bill. Following graduation in 1948, he moved to New York City, where he became a central figure of the New York School of Poetry. He received his doctorate at Columbia University and taught there for forty years. His course in imaginative writing proved a college highlight for many future writers. *Ko, or A Season on Earth*, a long poem in ottava rima, appeared in 1959; *Thank You and Other Poems* followed three years later. He adapted his teaching techniques to the needs of elementary school children and elderly residents of nursing homes, and worked a minor revolution in pedagogy through such influential books as *Rose, Where Did You Get That Red?* (1973) and *I Never Told Anybody* (1977). His recent collections of poetry include the posthumous *A Possible World* (2002), *New Addresses* (2000), *Straits* (1998), *One Train* (1994), and *On the Great Atlantic Rainway: Selected Poems 1950–1988* (1994), all from Knopf. Also published in the 1990s were two books about poetry: *The Art of Poetry* (University of Michigan, 1996) and *Making Your Own Days* (Scribner, 1998). He died in July 2002.

From the Brooklyn-based publishing house Soft Skull Press in 2004 appeared *The Art of the Possible*, a book of poetry comics, sometimes without pictures but with the other structural traits of comic books—the panel as a unit of composition, for example. Koch, who wanted to be a cartoonist when he was a kid, uses the comic strip to deal with "Civilization and its Discontents," in which twelve numbered hills surround a building marked "civilization" with a man, woman, and child in the vestibule. Below we are told to "see identification key on next page." There we encounter a sketch of a bearded and bespectacled face and the words "Key: The Mind of Sigmund Freud." Another series is "Dead White Man Comics." In the final one, you see a skeleton, a gravestone, and a person reading a book. And there's a defiant exclamatory cry: "If but one person reads me, than I am not really dead!!!"

JOHN KOETHE was born on December 25, 1945, in San Diego, California, and attended Princeton and Harvard universities. He has published six books of poetry, most recently *North Point North: New and Selected Poems* (HarperCollins, 2002). He teaches philosophy at the University of Wisconsin in Milwaukee.

Of "To an Audience," Koethe writes: "I heard an interview with a poet who said that he first tried to figure out what would appeal to an audience and then wrote to that. I was taken aback, since that's pretty much the opposite of the way I think of poems, which is basically as forms of talking to yourself (though I'm pleased if readers want to come along for the ride). But since I realized that that whole idea—talking to yourself—is problematic in various ways, I found myself thinking about a poem that would begin with it and then gradually dismantle it. I decided to write it in a somewhat declamatory style, and the tone I had in mind was close to that of Caliban's address to the audience in Auden's *The Sea and the Mirror*."

YUSEF KOMUNYAKAA was born in Bogalusa, Louisiana, in 1947. He enlisted in the United States Army in 1965 and was sent to Vietnam, where he served as a correspondent for (and later editor of) the military newspaper the *Southern Cross*. Educated at the University of Colorado, Colorado State University, and the University of California at Irvine, he is the author of *Pleasure Dome: New and Collected Poems, 1975–1999* (Wesleyan University Press, 2001), *Talking Dirty to the Gods* (Farrar, Straus and Giroux, 2000), and *Thieves of Paradise* (Wesleyan University Press, 1998). For *Neon Vernacular: New and Selected Poems, 1977–1989* he received the Pulitzer Prize. His prose is collected in *Blue Notes: Essays, Interviews & Commentaries*, which appeared in the Poets on Poetry Series (University of Michigan Press) in 2000. In collaboration with Sascha Feinstein he edited *The*

Jazz Poetry Anthology (Indiana University Press, 1991). He teaches at Princeton University. He was guest editor of *The Best American Poetry 2003*.

Asked by an interviewer "What is poetry?" Komunyakaa said, "Poetry is a kind of distilled insinuation."

SEAN MANZANO LABRADOR was born in an army hospital outside Honolulu, Hawaii, in December 1972. He graduated from Berkeley and is pursuing an MFA at San Francisco State. "When I go to the San Francisco Museum of Modern Art, I don't care about Chagall's cats," he notes. "I care about the sixty-plus-year-old Pinay and Pinoy Guardsmark guards guarding Chagall's cats. From there I write about how the artifice, the art, and the art lover collaborate in constructing anonymity and invisibility."

Of "The Dark Continent," Labrador writes: "The poem is part of an unpublished collection of interconnected metropolitan landscapes and how they overwhelm and deceive the reluctant poet with themes of moroseness and morbidity. What can a poet do but oblige? But the task taxes a poet's confidence in shaping the wor[l]d. The intersection is that retreat, that shudder and shutter, that conflict of poet wanting to create bright work out of fragments and shards. Silhouettes of lovers and memories of lovers populate the halfway houses and are witnesses to their own unfolding, aphasia, and sleeplessness. There is a logic and necessity to maintain their anonymity."

ANN LAUTERBACH was born in New York City in 1942. After college at the University of Wisconsin in Madison, she attended Columbia University on a Woodrow Wilson Fellowship, then moved to London, where she lived for seven years. On her return to the States, she worked for a number of years in art galleries in New York before she began teaching. Since 1991 she has been on the faculty of Bard College. She received a Guggenheim Fellowship in 1986 and a John D. and Catherine T. MacArthur Fellowship in 1993. Her books include *If in Time: Selected Poems, 1975–2000* (Penguin, 2001), *On a Stair* (Penguin, 1997), *And For Example* (Viking Penguin, 1994), *Clamor* (Viking Penguin, 1991), *Before Recollection* (Princeton University Press, 1987), and *Many Times, But Then* (University of Texas Press, 1979).

Lauterbach writes: "'After Mahler' is formally interested in ideas of scale, the way in which our linguistic focus shifts (detail to statement; detail as statement, and so forth) and as it does so, disturbs or ruptures the poem's vocabulary and topography. I had been thinking about the failure of hearing/listening in a culture that privileges visual over verbal communication, and how that failure is acted out as deafness to other cultures; how easy or convenient it is to omit 'their' details from 'our' intentions and actions. (My poetics is fundamentally an exploration of subjective, affective registers in relation to the possibilities for, and effects of, agency.) Gustav Mahler, the composer, represents for me a number of complex engagements with modernity in relation to lyricism, where lyricism is not simply a poetic mode, but a sign of linguistic specificity."

NATHANIEL MACKEY was born in Miami, Florida, in 1947. He is the author of three books of poetry: *Whatsaid Serif* (City Lights Books, 1998), *School of Udhra* (City Lights Books, 1993), and *Eroding Witness* (University of Illinois Press, 1985). *Strick: Song of the Andoumboulou 16–25,* a compact disc recording of poems read with musical accompaniment (Royal Hartigan, percussion; Hafez Modirzadeh, reeds and flutes), was released in 1995 by Spoken Engine Company. He is the author of a continuing prose composition, *From a Broken Bottle Traces of Perfume Still Emanate*, of which three volumes have thus far been published: *Bedouin Hornbook* (Callaloo Fiction Series, 1986; second edition: Sun and Moon Press, 1997), *Djbot Baghostus's Run* (Sun and Moon Press, 1993), and *Atet A.D.* (City Lights Books, 2001). He is the editor of the literary magazine *Hambone* and coeditor (with Art Lange) of the anthology *Moment's Notice: Jazz in Poetry and Prose* (Coffee House Press, 1993). He has also written a book of critical essays, *Discrepant Engagement: Dissonance, Cross-Culturality, and Experimental Writing* (Cambridge University Press, 1993). He is professor of literature at the University of California, Santa Cruz.

Mackey writes: "'Sound and Cerement' is a recent installment of '*Mu*,' a serial work named after trumpeter Don Cherry's albums '*Mu*' *First Part* and '*Mu*' *Second Part*. The series takes the seed-word *mu* as a 'note' common to *music, muse,* and *myth* (Jane Harrison's *muthos*: 'a re-utterance or pre-utterance, it is a focus of emotion'), lost ground and elegiac allure on the order of the Atlantis-like continent Mu. 'Sound and Cerement' is one of several poems in the series whose titles echo that of my essay 'Sound and Sentiment, Sound and Symbol,' an essay relating music, writing, and estrangement. 'Music is wounded kinship's last resort,' it says at one point."

HARRY MATHEWS was born in New York in 1930. His latest published book is *The Case of the Persevering Maltese: Collected Essays* (Dalkey Archive Press, 2003). Forthcoming is a memoir, *My Life in CIA: A Chronicle of 1973*, also to be published by Dalkey. He divides his time between Key West, Florida, and France.

Of "Lateral Disregard," Mathews writes: "The title is the philosopher Elaine Scarry's name for an aesthetic phenomenon: when we focus our attention on an object, its qualities are intensified, but our awareness of similar qualities in objects nearby is diminished.

"Kenneth Koch once remarked that he'd found a simple way of demonstrating that the beauty of poetry doesn't depend on its sound: change just one consonant in the opening line of a favorite Shakespeare sonnet, and its charm vanishes: 'Shall I compare thee to a summer's bay?'

"The altered verse did not strike me as devoid of poetic potential; there was also a temptation to challenge my friend's slightly cocky assumption that his demonstration was self-evident. In time I felt I must write a poem that started with the 'bay' variant, and so 'Lateral Disregard' came to be. Kenneth responded by saying that clearly his original statement had been proved wrong; I told him that was by no means true. It wasn't, in any case, the point: my opening line had led to a nostalgic recollection of life and love connected with 'a summer's bay' that I'd frequented many years before, and those had been my only concerns as I completed the poem."

STEVE MCCAFFERY was born in Sheffield, England, in 1947. He has written fifteen volumes of poetry, twenty chapbooks, and a novel, *Panopticon* (Blewointment Press, 1984). His poetry titles include *Bouma Shapes* (Zasterle Press, 2002) and *Seven Pages Missing*, 2 vols. (Coach House Press, 2001–2). His critical and theoretical writings include *North of Intention: Critical Writings, 1973–1986*

(Roof Books, 1986). He was a founding member with bp Nichol in 1972 of the TRG (Toronto Research Group), whose collected research reports he edited as *Rational Geomancy* (Talonbooks, 1992). He was for two notorious and legendary decades a member of the sound poetry ensemble The Four Horsemen and is currently David Gray Professor of Poetry and Letters at the State University of New York at Buffalo and director of the North American Centre for Interdisciplinary Poetics.

Of "Some Versions of Pastoral," McCaffery writes: "The title of this suite is directly appropriated from William Empson's great study of the pastoral, a work to which I allude both with homage and criticism. Absent from his study is what John Bull and John Barrell term the 'anti-pastoral' that flourished circa 1730–1850. Its practitioners and specimens include Stephen Duck's 'The Thresher's Labour,' Oliver Goldsmith's 'The Deserted Village,' George Crabbe's 'The Village,' William Holloway's 'The Peasant's Fate,' and Ebenezer Elliott, the Corn-Law Rhymer's 'The Splendid Village.' All in their different ways address the dark side of pastoral, the ideological undertones and lacunae beneath the utopia of the Theocritan idyll. It is a genre marked by death, whose primal scene is the murder of Abel, and whose haunting *ekphrasis* Poussin captures in his great painting *Et in Arcadia Ego*, anticipated two decades earlier in Guercino's *The Arcadian Shepherds* (1621). All the above informs and orchestrates my suite along with two questions: What is pastoral in an age of carcinomic neoliberalism and how do we address and utilize a defunct genre whose shards still carry such urgent pertinence?"

K. SILEM MOHAMMAD was born in Modesto, California, in 1962. He teaches English and writing at Southern Oregon University in Ashland. His books of poetry are *A Thousand Devils* (Combo Press, 2004), *Deer Head Nation* (Tougher Disguises Press, 2003), and *hovercraft* (Kenning Editions, 2000). He maintains a poetry and poetics blog entitled *lime tree* at limetree.ksilem.com.

On "Mars Needs Terrorists," Mohammad writes: "Like all the poems in *Deer Head Nation* (the book of which it is a part), this is an outgrowth of my involvement in a small e-mail-based poetry collective known as Flarf. Initiated by New York poet Gary Sullivan, Flarf began as a form whose chief aesthetic objective was to be as 'bad,' as 'offensive,' or (in Gary's words) as 'not OK' as possible. As Flarf evolved, in work by Sullivan, Jordan Davis, Katie Degentesh, Drew Gardner, Nada Gordon, and others, it began to include the practice of manipulating Google search result pages. 'Mars Needs Terrorists' resulted from a search for the string *terrorists, teenagers, wet, republican, sex,* and *slave*. It's one of the least-edited poems in *Deer Head Nation*, and hence one of the ones that most adheres to 'hard Flarf' (or perhaps 'deep Flarf') standards: I liked the sloppy, staticky quality of the phrases as they appeared largely at random after some initial trimming away of the Google headers and URLs and so on, wavering in and out of syntactic continuity like a frequently interrupted emergency broadcast transmitted over some alien channel. About all I did was to arrange the fragments in sonnet-length sections and add the alternating colons and periods at the beginning of each line. The poem is for me, finally, a formalized distress signal, an arational decoding of my traumatized affective response to both the terrorist attacks of 9/11 and Bush administration policy (the 'War on Terror,' the 'Patriot Act,' 'shock and awe,' etc.). The porn/spam elements just serve to catalyze the whole concoction into an (in)appropriately nauseous froth."

ERÍN MOURE was born in Calgary, Canada, in 1955. She has published ten books of poetry in Canada, most recently *O Cidadán* (House of Anansi Press, 2002; www.anansi.ca). Her translation from the Portuguese of Fernando Pessoa's *O Guardador de Rebanhos* appeared in 2001 under the title *Sheep's Vigil by a Fervent Person* (House of Anansi Press). She works as a freelance translator in Montreal.

Moure writes: "In my manuscript *Little Theatres*, '8 Little Theatres of the Cornices' is attributed to Elisa Sampedrín, who directed a small feminist theatre in the 1980s and '90s and is now, unjustly, nearly forgotten. In 1998 Sampedrín said: 'It's my hunch that in the next millennium, at least in its first years, hope is not going to count for much. That's when we'll most need little theatres. It's very conservative in its use of hope as fuel.'

"For my part, I might add that each of these little theatres of the cornices is intended to sit alone on its page; each piece is a little stage on which a small play takes place. I say this because the pieces will likely be broken across pages in this volume; the visual aspect of the writing will have vanished. You, reader, can imagine it as it should be."

PAUL MULDOON was born in County Armagh, Northern Ireland, in 1951, and was educated in Armagh and at the Queen's University of Belfast. From 1973 to 1986, he worked in Belfast as a radio and television producer for the British Broadcasting Corporation. Since 1987 he has lived in the United States, where he is now Howard G. B. Clark '21 University Professor in the Humanities at Princeton University. In 1999 he was elected professor of poetry at the University of Oxford. Muldoon's main collections of poetry are *Moy Sand and Gravel* (Farrar, Straus and Giroux, 2002), *Poems, 1968–1998* (Farrar, Straus and Giroux, 2001), *Hay* (Farrar, Straus and Giroux, 1998), *The Annals of Chile* (Farrar, Straus and Giroux, 1994), *Madoc: A Mystery* (Noonday Press, 1990), *Meeting the British* (Wake Forest University, 1987), *Quoof* (Wake Forest University, 1983), *Why Brownlee Left* (Wake Forest University, 1980), *Mules* (Faber and Faber, 1977), and *New Weather* (Faber and Faber, 1973). He won the 2003 Pulitzer Prize for Poetry.

Of "The Last Time I Saw Chris," Muldoon writes: "I wrote this poem as an 'assignment,' having set it for one of my classes at Princeton. The six end-words were chosen at random by six members of the class. I guessed I might be on to something when I discovered that there was indeed a gallery in Amagansett called the Crazy Monkey, 'monkey' being one of those end-words which didn't seem all that promising at first."

EILEEN MYLES was born in Cambridge, Massachusetts, in 1949. She is currently working on a new novel, *The Inferno*, and is collaborating with Los Angeles composer Michael Webster on an opera called *Hell*. Her most recent books are *on my way* (Faux Press, 2001) and *Skies* (Black Sparrow Press, 2001). She teaches at the University of California at San Diego.

Of "No Rewriting," Myles writes: "Feeling I'd be out of New York more than before, I wrote this poem collecting things about my life here. It was a lot longer but this was the good part. I went to a memorial event for Edward Said last week in San Diego and I liked what he said (in a book) about feeling that writing was his home. It's curious that some of us discovered both (home and writing) in New York and there's a lot of fear around picking it up and seeing what's living under its edges. I mean the identity of the writer who lives in New York. You can kind of scrape it up and look underneath. I am trying that now, but in this poem I was reeling in this building I had made."

ALICE NOTLEY was born in Bisbee, Arizona, in 1945. She is a full-time poet. She lives in Paris, France. Her most recent book of poetry is *Disobedience* (Penguin, 2001).

Of "State of the Union," Notley writes: "This work is part of a three-hundred-page manuscript called *Alma, or The Dead Women*, which is something like a novel and something like a poem, with characters, dialogue, singing, and invective. The title character of the whole manuscript, Alma, is god; she is a junky and shoots up in the center of her forehead, in order to dream and suffer the world's nightmare. 'State of the Union' itself was written at the time of the 2002 State of the Union address by the president, who is perceived finally as nothing but a set of genitals."

JENI OLIN was born in Houston, Texas, in 1974, the Year of the Tiger. She is the author of *The Heart's Filthy Lesson* (Angry Dog Press, 2001) and *A Valentine to Frank O'Hara* (Smokeproof Press, 1999). She studied at Oxford and Cambridge universities before receiving her BA and MFA from the Naropa Institute in Boulder, Colorado. She is studying at New York University to be a registered nurse. Her most recent title is the e-book *Blue Collar Holiday* (fauxpress.com).

Olin writes: "This poem takes place at 92 Little Plains Road in Southampton, Long Island, where I lived and worked with the late painter Larry Rivers for five years among the vitamin-stuffed bluebloods and Hampton-elite demimondes who 'slept their way to the middle.' Therefore, the title 'Blue Collar Holiday' is ironic. The 'Bad Secretary' piece mentioned in the poem depicts a turn-of-the-century businessman spanking his secretary over a desk and the foam-core bird paintings imitate the birds of the National Audubon Society Singing Bird Clock, such as the Tufted Titmouse and the White-breasted Nuthatch."

DANIELLE PAFUNDA was born in Albany, New York, in 1977. She attended Bard College and the graduate writing program at the New School University. Her first collection, *Pretty Young Thing,* is forthcoming from Soft Skull Press. She is coeditor of the online journal *La Petite Zine* and associate editor of *Verse*. She teaches at the University of Georgia.

Of "RSVP," Pafunda writes: "The ABC soap opera 'All My Children' made excessive use of the phrase 'pity party' during the summer of 2001, when I happened to be unemployed and watching like a fiend. 'Kill the people' is ripped off from *All About Eve*. As a whole, though, 'RSVP' sends my little regrets to that well-coiffed, ticky-tacky manifestation of the spectacle. At least this one time."

HEIDI PEPPERMINT was born in Dade County, Florida, in 1971. Her first collection of poems, *Guess Can Gallop*, was selected by Brenda Hillman as winner of the 2002 New Issues Poetry Prize. A founding editor of the literary magazine *Parakeet*, Peppermint has served as an assistant editor on *Salt Hill* and *Verse*. She is a part-time faculty member at Syracuse University.

Of "Real Toads," Peppermint writes: "The title references Marianne Moore's well-known admonition to poets to present 'imaginary gardens with real toads in them.' I read 'Real Toads,' in part, as an attempt to reckon with the ideas of 'masculine' and 'feminine' as they have been defined for me through language and association: I put 'Man' and 'Woman' in a room and let them do what my mind had been trained to have them do; then, I used this material as a point of departure into wordplay that sought to demythologize and reappropriate my imaginative space. This poem marks a shift in the relations between my 'She' and 'He.'"

BOB PERELMAN was born in Ohio in 1947. He attended the University of Michigan and the Writers' Workshop at the University of Iowa in 1971. In 1976 he moved from Cambridge, Massachusetts, to the San Francisco Bay Area, where he edited *Hills* magazine and organized the Talk Series and performances of the Zukofskys' *A-24*. In 1990 he received his PhD from Berkeley, and he now teaches at the University of Pennsylvania in Philadelphia. His sixteen books of poetry include *Ten to One: Selected Poems* (Wesleyan University Press, 1999) and *The Future of Memory* (Roof Books, 1998). His critical books are *The Marginalization of Poetry: Language Writing and Literary History* (Princeton University Press, 1996) and *The Trouble with Genius: Reading Pound, Joyce, Stein, and Zukofsky* (University of California Press, 1994).

Perelman writes: "'Here 2' receives its awkward title from the fact of its ancestor, my poem 'Here,' which I wrote over a decade and a half ago as part of *Face Value* (Roof Books, 1988). I never do this, recast a poem, but I did this time. A few old phrases remain. 'The Federal Building says Federal Building on the outside' is one I remember sparking this new poem when it struck me that I hadn't finished and can't yet finish addressing a condition that has been ours to live in since the 1980s at least: a global-disguised-as-local world where the language of power is both intrusively obvious and utterly opaque. 'We,' 'America,' 'freedom,' 'Iraq,' 'people'—those kinds of words almost always snap into mystery-patterns that, as they used to say of Britannia, rule the waves, only now the waves travel through air and space primarily and it's us (US of A) making the rulings, even though we didn't vote to act like this."

CARL PHILLIPS was born in Everett, Washington, in 1959. He is the author of seven books of poems, most recently *The Rest of Love* (Farrar, Straus and Giroux, 2004) and *Rock Harbor* (Farrar, Straus and Giroux, 2002). Other books include *Coin of the Realm: Essays on the Life and Art of Poetry* (Graywolf Press, 2004) and a translation of Sophocles' *Philoctetes* (Oxford, 2003). He teaches at Washington University in St. Louis.

Of "Pleasure," Phillips writes: "I'd been struggling with my version of writer's block. Having decided to give up for the day, I lay down and stared up at the sky through a skylight, one way of paying attention to the world and to how it continues whether or not we pay attention, whether we exist or not. It occurred to me that poetry, rather like the natural world, doesn't exist *for* us— we're not its purpose. If we're lucky, we get to make poems for a while, but we keep nothing in the end—that's, as I understand it, what comes with dying. Somehow, that line of thinking led to how desire in all of its forms gives inevitable shape to a life for better or, often, worse. I'd been working on an essay on the Psalms, which explains how the images of the bay tree and olive tree (from Psalms 37 and 52, respectively) crept in. As for the title: the pleasure in the act of making—with our minds as much as with our bodies—that, too, isn't ours. We'll have left it behind."

ROBERT PINSKY was born in Long Branch, New Jersey, in 1940. He is the author of six books of poems, most recently *Jersey Rain* (Farrar, Straus and Giroux, 2000), and translator of *The Inferno of Dante*. As United States Poet Laureate, he started the Favorite Poem Project, and he continues his work on this audio and video archive featuring Americans from all walks of life reading aloud beloved poems. He is the poetry editor of *Slate* magazine and a regular contributor to *The NewsHour with Jim Lehrer* on PBS. He teaches in the graduate writing program at Boston University.

Pinsky writes: "'Samba' tries to engage the accelerated connections of New York, the city's mishmash glamour and free-swinging eclecticism. For me growing up in Long Branch, New Jersey, it was not a city but The City, the place where movies happen. Movies, and movement. The restless motion of New York for me contains a hopeful quality, redeeming the speed of change, a cosmopolitan gesture against nativism, against provincialism, against imperialism itself, without self-righteousness but with a brisk, humane, polyglot force from right within the Empire State. That busy, transcendental, everyday liberty is what the poem tries to track."

CARL RAKOSI was born in Berlin, Germany, in 1903. From 1904 to 1910, he lived with his grandparents before coming to the United States. He was educated at the University of Wisconsin in Madison and at the University of Pennsylvania, where he received a master's degree in social work. Until his retirement in 1966, he practiced social work and psychotherapy in New York, Boston, Cleveland, Chicago, New Orleans, St. Louis, and Minneapolis. He also taught school in Houston and worked as an industrial psychologist in Milwaukee. His poems first appeared in the *Little Review*—where Joyce, Eliot, Pound, and Hemingway were first published—and in Ezra Pound's *The Exile*, of which there were only four issues. In the early 1930s, he was associated with the Objectivists. His recent books include *The Old Poet's Tale* (Etruscan Books, 1999), *The Earth Suite* (Etruscan Books, 1997), *Poems, 1923–1941* (Sun and Moon Press, 1995), and *Collected Poetry* (National Poetry Foundation, 1986). Carl Rakosi died at home in San Francisco on June 25, 2004, following a series of strokes. He was one hundred years old.

Rakosi writes: "The idea for 'In the First Circle of Limbo' came from my perception that categorizing is a seductive process, that it serves a very specific, practical function, but that for other functions, especially in the arts, it is much too limiting and tends to hold one in bondage."

ED ROBERSON was born in Pittsburgh, Pennsylvania, in 1939. His books include *Atmosphere Conditions* (Sun and Moon Press, 2000), *Just In: Word of Navigational Challenges: New and Selected Work* (Talisman House Press, 1998), *Voices Cast Out to Talk Us In* (University of Iowa Press, 1995), and *When Thy King Is a Boy* (University of Pittsburgh Press, 1970). He has received a Lila Wallace–Reader's Digest Writer's Award.

Of "Ideas Gray Suits Bowler Hats Baal," Roberson writes: "The idea that god required human blood sacrifice always seemed counter to the idea of god to me. Ripping out people's hearts and rolling them down the stairs, throwing children into fires and including to this day all the acts perpetrated against virgins—all to be received as gifts of devotion—just never seemed very godlike or even acceptable to anything godlike.

"If it is possible to get angry with humankind, then you can say we had words. If those words can get ugly, then this is ugly. This poem was written in anger. I suppose in the tradition of the cosmic complaint. It's just that I have kids—girls—and I love them."

KIT ROBINSON was born in Evanston, Illinois, in 1949. He graduated from Yale College in 1971, moved to the San Francisco Bay Area, and has lived there ever since. Seventeen books of his poetry have appeared, including the recent *9:45* (The Post-Apollo Press, 2003) and *The Crave* (Atelos Press, 2002). His translation of Ilya Kutik's *Ode on Visiting the Belosaraisk Spit on the Sea of Azov* (Aleph Books, 1995) followed a trip to Russia in 1990. He is currently self-employed as a communications consultant.

Robinson writes: "'The 3D Matchmove Artist' was written after viewing *Men in Black II* on a plane from New York to San Francisco on November 11, 2002. The title is taken from the film credits. The poem wrote itself quickly and no revisions were made."

CARLY SACHS was born in 1979 and grew up in Youngstown, Ohio. She attended Kent State University and the graduate writing program at New School University. She has taught English at Walton High School in the Bronx and now works in Washington, D.C.

Of "The Story," Sachs writes: "This poem started off as an exercise in revisiting a memory. The poem is about survival and illustrates how the recall of a painful incident changes over time. In this case, the speaker regains the power to take charge of her words and rearrange them, supplanting the original version of events. It is a reclaiming of language, a revision of a memory, a rebuilding of the body. Yet, in a way, the shame is evident, as the memory's linear narrative is concealed, while at other points of time, the raw, jagged things that make language visceral are exposed."

JENNIFER SCAPPETTONE was born in Bayshore, New York, in 1972. She is a doctoral candidate at the University of California at Berkeley.

Of "III," Scappettone writes: "When the poem was written (just after the non-apocalypse of triple zeros struck), I was reading or rereading Thomas Wyatt, Gaspara Stampa, Charles Chesnutt's *The Conjure Woman,* John Ruskin's *Fors Clavigera: Letters to the Workmen and Labourers of Great Britain,* and Walter Benjamin's 'Central Park.'"

FREDERICK SEIDEL was born in St. Louis, Missouri, in 1936. He attended Harvard College. His books of poems include *Final Solutions* (Random House, 1963), *Sunrise* (Viking, 1980), *These Days* (Knopf, 1989), *Poems, 1959–1979* (Knopf, 1989), *My Tokyo* (1993), *Going Fast* (2000), *The Cosmos Poems* (2001), *Life on Earth* (2001), and *Area Code 212* (2002). These last three have recently been brought together in a single volume, *The Cosmos Trilogy* (2003). Since 1993 he has been published by Farrar, Straus and Giroux.

DAVID SHAPIRO was born in Newark, New Jersey, in 1947. A professional violinist in his youth, he attended Columbia University, won a Kellett Fellowship to Cambridge University, and edited, with Ron Padgett, *An Anthology of New York Poets* (Random House, 1970). His early books are *January* (Holt, Rinehart and Winston, 1965), *Poems from Deal* (Dutton, 1969), and *A Man Holding an Acoustic Panel* (Dutton, 1971). More recent titles include *House (Blown Apart)* (1988), *After a Lost Original* (1994), and *A Burning Interior* (2002), all published by Overlook Press. He is an art historian at William Paterson University and also has taught for twenty-five years at the Cooper Union. His monument for Palach with John Hejduk was dedicated in Prague by President Vaclav Havel.

Shapiro writes: "It took me many years to assemble, erase, and tear 'A Burning Interior.' Many of my long sequences have such a fate. Here, parts of the poem and the order kept changing, turning slowly into an elegy and a celebration of architecture. 'Light Bulb' and other parts owe their existence to those who set the highest standards: Jasper Johns and his sculpture, Meyer Schapiro, who let me listen to his golden voice, and the late Kenneth Koch. I hope always to aspire to Kenneth's sense of freshness and the search for happiness. He always wanted me to write long poems, and yet he did not like willful extensions. This poem therefore joins the long poems I have written since childhood, at least one in each of my books. I hope it is not merely a suite, but a divertimento."

RON SILLIMAN was born in Pasco, Washington, in 1946. He grew up in Berkeley, California, and now lives in Chester County, Pennsylvania, and works as a market analyst in the computer industry. He has written and edited twenty-five books, including the anthology *In the American Tree* (National Poetry Foundation, 2001). Since 1979 he has been writing a poem entitled *The Alphabet*. Volumes from that project published thus far include ® (Drogue Press, 1999), *What* (The Figures, 1998), *Xing* (Meow Press, 1996), *N/O* (Roof Press, 1994), *Jones* (Generator Press, 1993), *Demo to Ink* (Chax Press, 1992), *Toner* (Potes & Poets Press, 1992), *Manifest* (Zasterle Press, 1990), *Lit* (Potes & Poets Press, 1987), *Paradise* (Burning Deck, 1985), and *ABC* (Tuumba Press, 1983). Cuneiform Press will publish *Woundwood*, a section of *VOG*, in 2004.

Silliman writes: "'Compliance Engineering' is the second poem from *VOG* to be chosen for *The Best American Poetry* series (see 'For Larry Eigner, Silent' in the 2002 edition). *VOG* is one section of a much longer poem, *The Alphabet*, and is distinct from the others in that work by being, as near as possible, an 'ordinary book of poems,' something I haven't attempted since my college days in the 1960s. 'Compliance Engineering' attempts to construct itself around familiar objects, scenes, and comments. *VOG* is an acronym common in TV scripts for the off-screen announcer (such as Don Pardo on *Saturday Night Live*). These days, the acronym stands for Voice-Over Guy, but in the 1950s, it stood for Voice of God."

BRUCE SMITH was born in Philadelphia, Pennsylvania, in 1946. He is the author of four books of poems: *The Other Lover* (University of Chicago Press, 2000), *Mercy Seat* (University of Chicago Press, 1994), *Silver and Information* (National Poetry Series Selection, University of Georgia Press, 1985), and *The Common Wages* (Sheep Meadow Press, 1985). He teaches in the graduate writing program at Syracuse University.

Of "Song of the Ransom of the Dark," Smith writes: "Two voices at odds with one another. One in the dark at the wrecked and splendid spectacle of a movie and the other in a foreign country in order to adopt a child. From the divergence and harmony of these two voices, a third thing."

BRIAN KIM STEFANS was born in Rutherford, New Jersey, in 1969. He is a part-time web editor for the CUNY Graduate Center, a freelance book reviewer, erstwhile net artist (his works are collected at www.arras.net, a site devoted to "new media poetry and poetics"), and an aspiring playwright. His books include *Fashionable Noise: On Digital Poetics* (Atelos Press, 2003), *Angry Penguins* (Harry Tankoos Books, 2000), *Gulf* (Object Editions, 1998), and *Free Space Comix* (Roof Books, 1998).

Of "They're Putting a New Door In," Stefans writes: "The poem tells the story of its own writing quite accurately: the last month of the year, lots of noise and chatter in my apartment as my superintendent, Eliot, and an assistant were installing a spanking new white door, a real bargain basement one that was intended for the front porch of a prefab suburban house with an Italianate flair and not a Williamsburg apartment in a state of near collapse. There's a line from John Ashbery and Joe Brainard's *Vermont Notebook* in there—I think the openness and modesty of that funky little collaboration beneficially influenced this poem. I felt free to drop things in there (aborted poem ideas, the loose quatrain), so the stress index is probably a little lower than usual for me, a counterpoint to the sort of grim assessment of the beginning of the new Dark Ages that the poem professes to be about. I should also mention that I'd written more than three poems in 2001, but this is the one that makes them smile."

GERALD STERN was born in Pittsburgh, Pennsylvania, in 1925, and was educated at the University of Pittsburgh and Columbia University. He has written thirteen books of poetry including *This Time: New and Selected Poems*, which won the National Book Award in 1998, and most recently *American Sonnets* (2002), both from W. W. Norton. A collection of personal essays titled *What I Can't Bear Losing: Notes from a Life* was released by Norton in 2003. A Guggenheim Fellow, he was the first Poet Laureate of New Jersey, serving from 2000 to 2002.

Of "Dog That I Am," Stern writes: "This poem is about a failed love affair in St. Louis (Skinker is the name of a St. Louis street), and a considerable portion of it constitutes a description of the 'beloved.' But it is the *nature* of the relationship—as seen in the poem—that is a little vague (to me). Certainly I (the speaker) was her 'dog,' but the dog becomes quickly universal and metaphysical. I think I saw somebody with a small dog, here in Lambertville, New Jersey, that looked like her, coat, hair, and all; I always *start* with the literal. In actuality, her dog at the time, her real dog, was an overweight German shepherd who sat on the first landing with his teeth bared. It was hard getting up those stairs, and I always hated that dog—probably the only dog I ever hated."

VIRGIL SUÁREZ was born in Havana, Cuba, in 1962. He has lived in the United States since 1974. His books include *Infinite Refuge* (Arte Publico Press, 2002), *Palm Crows* (University of Arizona Press, 2001), *Banyan* (Louisiana State University Press, 2001), and *Guide to the Blue Tongue* (University of Illinois Press, 2002). In 2005 the University of Pittsburgh Press will publish *90 Miles: Selected and New Poems*. He is coeditor of four anthologies published by the University of Iowa Press: *American Diaspora* (2001); *Like Thunder* (2002); *Vespers* (2003); and *Red, White, and Blue* (2004). He is currently writing a new novel and restoring a '55 Chevrolet. He lives and works in Florida and loves the great city of Miami.

Of *"La Florida,"* Suárez writes: "I moved to Florida in 1987 and have lived in both Coral Gables and Key Biscayne all these years. They are great places for the study of tropical fauna and flora. I've always considered myself an urban poet, but the natural world cannot be avoided here in Florida. Nature is constant, it is out there—that's what the poem builds upon. When I was a teenager I used to fish near the Everglades, and I'd watch the alligators float by. Egrets catching sun in their wings. Fish jumping every so often. Nature teaches you how to let go, how to commune, how to visualize that which happens even when you are no longer present."

ARTHUR SZE was born in New York City in 1950. Among his seven books of poetry are *The Silk Dragon: Translations from the Chinese* (2001), *The Redshifting Web: Poems, 1970–1998* (1998), and *Archipelago* (1995), all from Copper Canyon Press. A recipient of a Lila Wallace–Reader's Digest Writer's Award and a Guggenheim Fellowship, he teaches at the Institute of American Indian Arts in Santa Fe, New Mexico.

Of "Acanthus," Sze writes: "Notes about poems are just notes; but I'd like to mention that my wife, Carol Moldaw, and I were traveling from Istanbul down the Aegean Coast with Nezih Onur, who translated our poetry into Turkish. Although many of the images come from this journey—*raki* is an aniseed liqueur that turns cloudy-white when one pours water into it—the impulse to the poem is to close one's eyes in order to see."

JAMES TATE was born in Kansas City, Missouri, in 1943. His *Selected Poems* (Wesleyan University Press) won the 1991 Pulitzer Prize. *Worshipful Company of Fletchers* (Ecco) won the National Book Award in 1994. Among his recent books are *Memoir of the Hawk* (2001) and *Shroud of the Gnome* (1997), both from Ecco/HarperCollins. He teaches at the University of Massachusetts in Amherst and was the guest editor of *The Best American Poetry 1997*.

Tate writes: "'Bounden Duty' is based on a true incident. I had first met President Clinton when he was still in high school. His girlfriend had dragged him to a poetry reading I was giving in Little Rock. I met them and chatted with them briefly at the party afterwards. I was struck by the force of his personality. I think her name was Gigi. Years later, I was one of many poets invited to the White House. The president acted as if we were old friends. I was flattered, but also suspicious. Several months later I got the call. He still sends me Christmas cards, but I fear that I let him down in some small way."

EDWIN TORRES was born in the Bronx in 1958. His titles include *Please* (CD-Rom from Faux Press, 2002), *The All-Union Day of the Shock Worker* (Roof Books, 2001), and *Fractured Humorous* (Subpress, 1999). His performance work has brought him into collaborations with the musician Sean G. Meehan, the Nurse Kaya String Quartet, and DJ Spooky. His poetry CDs are *Novo* (OozeBap Records, 2003; www.oozebap.org) and *Holy Kid* (Kill Rock Stars, 1998), which was part of the Whitney Museum's "The American Century, 1950–2000" exhibit. He is coeditor of the literary journal *Rattapallax*. He works as a graphic designer and lives in the East Village in New York City.

Of "The Theorist Has No Samba!" Torres writes: "The poem is from an e-mail exchange with the poet Tom Devaney. It's unchanged, one of those creatures that flows out in a flurry with nary a thought to intrude on the thought. During an improvisation the energy guided by personal history creates its own moment, an understanding that there are things out of my control and what I need to do is step aside and trust that energy or at least its direction. So I've been interested in how poetry can allow that sort of spontaneity to create evolutions of spontaneity. And that morning, that instant, the idea of the instant sort of congealed into a Futurist bafflement of possible theory. And in this analysis of that instant, I've put more thought on what was meant to be a fleeting thought, now captured, here, forever."

RODRIGO TOSCANO was born in San Diego, California, in 1964. He lived in San Francisco from 1995 to 1999 and now lives in New York City. His books of poetry are *To Leveling Swerve* (Krupskaya Books, 2004), *Platform* (Atelos Press, 2003), *The Disparities* (Green Integer Books, 2002), and *Partisans* (O Books, 1999). His poetry has been translated into German, Spanish, Portuguese, and Catalan.

Toscano writes: "'Meditatio Lectoris' simultaneously engages several dimensions of a typical poetry reading as practiced in the U.S. The site of the event itself is raised to a status of collective activism through an analogy of shared work between reader and audience. Meaning-making is fundamentally figured as a proletarian activity (variously fettered, variously liberated)—one fraught with ideological-aesthetic risks on all sides. Highlighted throughout the poem is the (social) anxiety that comes from such a cultural exchange, a kind of from-the-get-go content."

PAUL VIOLI was born in New York in 1944. His books of poems include *Breakers* (2000), a selection of long poems, from Coffee House Press; and *Fracas* (1999), *Likewise* (1998), and *The Curious Builder* (1993), all from Hanging Loose Press, which also published his book of short nonfiction, *Selected Accidents, Pointless Anecdotes* (2002). He teaches at Columbia University, New York University, and the graduate writing program at New School University.

Of "Appeal to the Grammarians," Violi writes: "The last seven lines of the poem are directly quoted from my journal. It is the only entry for May 14, 1997. I didn't expect the incident to lead to a poem, but it did leave me wanting to say something about speechlessness and make something out of it perhaps, a self-portrait, a nonplussed cartoon character with a bubble caption overhead punctured by a gigantic exclamation point. Over the next two years, other thoughts came into play: I recalled that the first time I read Spanish I assumed the inverted exclamation point at the beginning of a sentence signaled that a startling disappointment was on the way. I learned later that the Royal Spanish Academy mandated the use of it in the mid-eighteenth century, and then I imagined a lengthy addition to Fowler's indicating when such a versatile mark would be appropriate. When that list got out of hand, I reduced it to a simple request."

DAVID WAGONER was born in Massillon, Ohio, in 1926. He has published seventeen books of poems, most recently *The House of Song* (University of Illinois

Press, 2002), and ten novels, one of which, *The Escape Artist*, was made into a movie by Francis Ford Coppola. Wagoner was a chancellor of the Academy of American Poets for twenty-three years. He has taught at the University of Washington since 1954 and was the editor of *Poetry Northwest* until it ceased publication in 2002.

Of "Trying to Make Music," Wagoner writes: "When I quit smoking long ago, I had even more trouble concentrating while trying to write poems. When I discovered earplugs, the tobacco part of the problem disappeared, and I had only the many noises and voices in my mind's ear to contend with. This poem and Pasternak's comment describe some of those. I've been inside a number of mental and penal institutions (always as a visitor so far) and have listened to gibberish of many kinds, to the radio, TV, and cocktail party versions too, and to bad music of many varieties, and I've often been reminded of their resemblance to what gets between me and my poems."

CHARLES WRIGHT was born in Pickwick Dam, Tennessee, in 1935, and was educated at Davidson College and the University of Iowa. His recent books of poems, all from Farrar, Straus and Giroux, include *Buffalo Yoga* (2004), *Negative Blue* (2000), *Appalachia* (1998), *Black Zodiac* (1997), and *Chickamauga* (1995). *Black Zodiac* won the Pulitzer Prize and the *Los Angeles Times* Book Prize. *Chickamauga* won the Lenore Marshall Prize. In 1999 he was elected a chancellor of the Academy of American Poets. He teaches at the University of Virginia in Charlottesville.

Of "In Praise of Han Shan," Wright writes: "Endgame. Last poem in a book, *Buffalo Yoga*, poet subsumed by his subject matter, leaving hieroglyphs from one on the hieroglyphs of the other. Art for nothing's sake."

MAGAZINES WHERE THE POEMS
WERE FIRST PUBLISHED

American Poetry Review, eds. Stephen Berg, David Bonanno, and Arthur Vogelsang. 1721 Walnut St., Philadelphia, PA 19103.

Antennae, ed. Jesse Seldess. 851 N. Hoyne Ave., #3R, Chicago, IL 60622.

Aufgabe, ed. E. Tracy Grinnell. 97 Summit St., #3, Brooklyn, NY 11231.

Boston Review, poetry eds. Mary Jo Bang and Timothy Donnelly. E53-407, MIT, 30 Wadsworth St., Cambridge, MA 02139-4307.

The Butcher Shop, eds. Simon Morrison, Sarah Norek, and Kristen Shaw. English Department, Macalester College, 1600 Grand Ave., St. Paul, MN 55105.

Can We Have Our Ball Back?, ed. Jim Behrle. www.canwehaveourballback.com.

The Canary, eds. Joshua Edwards, Anthony Robinson, and Nick Twemlow. canaryriver@yahoo.com.

Chicago Review, poetry ed. Eric P. Elshtain. 5801 South Kenwood Ave., Chicago, IL 60637.

Columbia Poetry Review, English Department, Columbia College, 600 South Michigan Ave., Chicago, IL 60605.

Conduit, ed. William D. Waltz. 510 8th Ave. NE, Minneapolis, MN 55413.

Conjunctions, ed. Bradford Morrow. 21 E. 10th St., New York, NY 10003.

DCPoetry Anthology 2003, ed. Tom Orange. www.dcpoetry.com/anth2003.htm.

Ecopoetics, ed. Jonathan Skinner. 106 Huntington Ave., Buffalo, NY 14214.

Exquisite Corpse, ed. Andrei Codrescu. www.corpse.org.

Fence, poetry eds. Caroline Crumpacker, Matthew Rohrer, and Max Winter. 303 E. 8th St., #B1, New York, NY 10003.

Five Points, eds. David Bottoms and Megan Sexton. Georgia State University, 33 Gilmer St. SE, Unit 8, Atlanta, GA 30303-3088.

The Forward, poetry ed. Rodger Kamenetz. 45 E. 33rd St., New York, NY 10016.

Fulcrum, eds. Philip Nikolayev and Katia Kapovich. 334 Harvard St., Suite D-2, Cambridge, MA 02139.

Green Mountains Review, ed. Neil Shepard. Johnson State College, Johnson, VT 05656.

Hanging Loose, eds. Robert Hershon, Dick Lourie, Mark Pawlak, and Ron Schreiber. 231 Wyckoff St., Brooklyn, NY 11217.

Harper's Magazine, ed. Lewis H. Lapham. 666 Broadway, New York, NY 10012.

Hotel Amerika, ed. David Lazar. Ohio University, English Department, 360 Ellis Hall, Athens, OH 45701.

Jacket, ed. John Tranter. jacketmagazine.com.

Kiosk: A Journal of Poetry, Poetics & Prose, eds. Gordon Hadfield, Sasha Steensen, and Kyle Schlesinger. State University of New York at Buffalo, Samuel Clemens Hall, Rm. 306, Buffalo, NY 14260-4610. wings.buffalo.edu/epc/mags/kiosk/.

La Petite Zine, eds. Jeffrey Salane and Danielle Pafunda. www.lapetitezine.org/.

Lyric, poetry ed. Eve Grubin. PO Box 980814, Houston, TX 77098.

Manoa, ed. Frank Stewart. Dept. of English, University of Hawaii, 1733 Donaghho Rd., Honolulu, HI 96822.

Michigan Quarterly Review, ed. Laurence Goldstein. 3574 Rackham Bldg., 915 E. Washington St., Ann Arbor, MI 48109-1070.

Mississippi Review, guest ed. Angela Ball. University of Southern Mississippi, Box 5144, Hattiesburg, MS 39406-5144.

New American Writing, eds. Paul Hoover and Maxine Chernoff. 369 Molino Ave., Mill Valley, CA 94941.

New England Review, poetry ed. C. Dale Young. Middlebury College, Middlebury, VT 05753.

The New Republic, poetry ed. Glyn Maxwell. 1331 H St. NW, Ste. 700, Washington, DC 20005.

The New Yorker, poetry ed. Alice Quinn. 4 Times Square, New York, NY 10036.

No: a journal of the arts, eds. Ben Lerner and Deb Klowden. 39 W. 29th St., #11A, New York, NY 10001.

Open City, eds. Thomas Beller and Joanna Yas. 270 Lafayette St., Ste. 1412, New York, NY 10012.

Pataphysics, eds. Leo Edelstein and Yanni Florence. PO Box 6054, St. Kilda Rd. Central, Melbourne 8008, Australia.

Pleiades, poetry ed. Wayne Miller. Department of English and Philosophy, Central Missouri State University, Warrensburg, MO 64093.

Ploughshares, poetry ed. David Daniel. Emerson College, 100 Beacon St., Boston, MA 02116.

PMS, ed. Linda Frost. University of Alabama at Birmingham, Department of English, 217 Humanities Bldg., 900 South 13th St., Birmingham, AL 35294-1260.

Poetry Daily, eds. Rob Anderson, Diane Boller, and Don Selby. www.poems.com.

POOL: A Journal of Poetry, eds. Amy Schroeder and Judith Taylor. PO Box 49738, Los Angeles, CA 90049.

Provincetown Arts, ed. Christopher Busa. PO Box 35, 650 Commercial St., Provincetown, MA 02657.

Rapidfeed, ed. Mike San Yup Kim. Mea Culpa Press, 2018 Shattuck Ave., PMB 103, Berkeley, CA 94704.

Rattapallax, eds. Edwin Torres and Flávia Rocha. 532 La Guardia Place, Ste. 353, New York, NY 10012.

Sal Mimeo, ed. Larry Fagin. 437 E. 12th St., #18, New York, NY 10009.

SHINY, ed. Michael Friedman. PO Box 13125, Denver, CO 80201.

The Threepenny Review, poetry ed. Wendy Lesser. PO Box 9131, Berkeley, CA 94709.

Tin House, poetry ed. Amy Bartlett. 2601 PO Box 10500, Portland, OR 97210.

TriQuarterly, ed. Susan Firestone Hahn. 2020 Ridge Ave., Evanston, IL 60208-4302.

26: A Journal of Poetry and Poetics, eds. Avery Burns, Rusty Morrison, Joseph Noble, Elizabeth Robinson, and Brian Strang. PO Box 4450, Saint Mary's College, Moraga, CA 94575-4730.

Van Gogh's Ear, ed. Ian Ayres. PO Box 582, Stuyvesant Station, New York, NY 10009.

ACKNOWLEDGMENTS

The series editor wishes to thank Mark Bibbins for his invaluable assistance. Angela Ball, Shanna Compton, Kim Gek Lin Harrison, Stacey Harwood, Danielle Pafunda, Karl Parker, John Schertzer, Michael Schiavo, and Susan Wheeler made useful suggestions. Warm thanks go also to Glen Hartley, Lynn Chu, and Katy Sprinkel of Writers' Representatives, and to Alexis Gargagliano, Cristine LeVasser, Erich Hobbing, and John McGhee of Scribner.

Grateful acknowledgment is made of the magazines in which these poems first appeared and the magazine editors who selected them. A sincere attempt has been made to locate all copyright holders. Unless otherwise noted, copyright to the poems is held by the individual poets.

Kim Addonizio: "Chicken" appeared in *Five Points*. Reprinted by permission of the poet.

Will Alexander: from "Solea of the Simooms" appeared in *No: a journal of the arts*. Reprinted by permission of the poet.

Bruce Andrews: from "Dang Me," appeared in *SHINY*. Reprinted by permission of the poet.

Rae Armantrout: "Almost" from *Up to Speed*. Copyright © 2004 by Rae Armantrout. Reprinted by permission of the poet and Wesleyan University Press. First appeared in *Mississippi Review*.

Craig Arnold: "Your friend's arriving on the bus" appeared in *Open City*. Reprinted by permission of the poet.

John Ashbery: "Wolf Ridge" appeared in *Conjunctions*. Reprinted by permission of the poet.

Mary Jo Bang: "The Eye Like a Strange Balloon Mounts Toward Infinity" appeared in *Ploughshares*. Reprinted by permission of the poet.

Alan Bernheimer: "20 Questions," appeared in *SHINY* and the *Forward*. Reprinted by permission of the poet.

Charles Bernstein: "Sign Under Test" appeared in *Michigan Quarterly Review*. Reprinted by permission of the poet.

Anselm Berrigan: "Token Enabler" appeared in *Rattapallax, Mississippi Review*, and *Can We Have Our Ball Back?* Reprinted by permission of the poet.

Mark Bibbins: from "Blasted Fields of Clover Bring Harrowing and Regretful Sighs" from *Sky Lounge*. Copyright © 2003 by Mark Bibbins. Reprinted by permission of the poet and Graywolf Press. First appeared in *Boston Review*.

Oni Buchanan: "The Walk" from *What Animal*. Copyright © 2003 by Oni Buchanan. Reprinted by permission of the poet and the University of Georgia Press. First appeared in *Conduit*.

Michael Burkard: "a cloud of dusk" appeared in *Lyric*. Reprinted by permission of the poet.

Anne Carson: "Gnosticism" appeared in the *New Yorker*. Reprinted by permission; copyright © 2003 by Anne Carson.

T. J. Clark: "Landscape with a Calm" appeared in the *Threepenny Review*. Reprinted by permission of the poet.

Billy Collins: "The Centrifuge" appeared in *Fulcrum*. Reprinted by permission of the poet.

Jack Collom: "3-4-00" appeared in *Ecopoetics*. Reprinted by permission of the poet.

Michael Costello: "Ode to My Flint and Boom Bolivia" appeared in *Columbia Poetry Review*. Reprinted by permission of the poet.

Michael Davidson: "Bad Modernism" appeared in *No: a journal of the arts*. Reprinted by permission of the poet.

Olena Kalytiak Davis: "You Art A Scholar, Horatio, Speak To It" from *shattered sonnets love cards and other off and back handed importunities*. Copyright © 2003 by Olena Kalytiak Davis. Reprinted by permission of the poet and Bloomsbury USA. First appeared in *Tin House*.

Jean Day: "Prose of the World Order" appeared in *26: A Journal of Poetry and Poetics*. Reprinted by permission of the poet.

Linh Dinh: "13" from *Blood and Soap*. Copyright © 2004 by Linh Dinh. Reprinted by permission of the poet and Seven Stories Press. First appeared in *American Poetry Review*.

Rita Dove: "All Souls'" appeared in the *New Yorker*. Reprinted by permission; copyright © 2003 by Rita Dove.

Rachel Blau DuPlessis: "Draft 55: Quiptych" from *Conjunctions*. Reprinted by permission of the poet.

kari edwards: "short sorry" from *iduna* (O Books). Copyright © 2003 by kari edwards. Reprinted by permission. First appeared in *Aufgabe*.

Kenward Elmslie: "Sibling Rivalry" from *New American Writing*. Reprinted by permission of the poet.

Aaron Fogel: "337,000, December, 2000" appeared in *Pataphysics*. Reprinted by permission of the poet.

Arielle Greenberg: "Saints" appeared in the *Canary*. Reprinted by permission of the poet.

Ted Greenwald: "Anyway" appeared in *SHINY*. Reprinted by permission of the poet.

Barbara Guest: "Nostalgia of the Infinite" appeared in *No: a journal of the arts*. Reprinted by permission of the poet.

Carla Harryman: from "Baby" appeared in *Sal Mimeo*. Reprinted by permission of the poet.

Jane Hirshfield: "Poe: An Assay (I)" appeared in the *Threepenny Review*. Reprinted by permission of the poet.

John Hollander: "For 'Fiddle-De-Dee'" appeared in *Hotel Amerika*. Reprinted by permission of the poet.

Fanny Howe: "Catholic" from *The Wedding Dress*. Copyright © 2003 by Fanny Howe. Reprinted by permission of the poet and the University of California Press. First appeared in *Chicago Review*.

Kenneth Irby: "[Record]" appeared in *No: a journal of the arts*. Reprinted by permission of the poet.

Major Jackson: from "Urban Renewal" appeared in *Provincetown Arts* and *Poetry Daily*. Reprinted by permission of the poet.

Marc Jaffee: "King of Repetition" appeared in *Hanging Loose*. Reprinted by permission of the poet.

Kenneth Koch: "The Man" appeared in *SHINY*. Reprinted by permission of the Estate of Kenneth Koch.

John Koethe: "To an Audience" appeared in *TriQuarterly*. Reprinted by permission of the poet.

Yusef Komunyakaa: "Ignis Fatuus" appeared in the *New Republic*. Reprinted by permission of the poet.

Sean Manzano Labrador: "The Dark Continent" appeared in *Rapidfeed*. Reprinted by permission of the poet.

Ann Lauterbach: "After Mahler" appeared in *No: a journal of the arts*. Reprinted by permission of the poet.

Nathaniel Mackey: "Sound and Cerement" appeared in *Hotel Amerika*. Reprinted by permission of the poet.

Harry Mathews: "Lateral Disregard" appeared in *SHINY* and *Jacket*. Reprinted by permission of the poet.

Steve McCaffery: "Some Versions of Pastoral" from *Bouma Shapes* (Zasterle Press). Copyright © 2002 by Steve McCaffery. Reprinted by permission of the poet. Also appeared in *TriQuarterly*.

K. Silem Mohammad: "Mars Needs Terrorists" from *Deer Head Nation*. Copyright © 2003 by K. Silem Mohammad. Reprinted by permission of Tougher Disguises. First appeared in *Kiosk*.

Erín Moure: "8 Little Theatres of the Cornices" from *No: a journal of the arts*. Reprinted by permission of the poet.

Paul Muldoon: "The Last Time I Saw Chris" appeared in the *New Yorker*. Reprinted by permission; copyright © 2003 by Paul Muldoon.

Eileen Myles: "No Rewriting" appeared in *Mississippi Review*. Reprinted by permission of the poet.

Alice Notley: "State of the Union" appeared in *Columbia Poetry Review*. Reprinted by permission of the poet.

Jeni Olin: "Blue Collar Holiday" appeared in *Hanging Loose*, *Exquisite Corpse*, and *Jacket*. Reprinted by permission of the poet.

Danielle Pafunda: "RSVP" appeared in *Pleiades*. Reprinted by permission of the poet.

Heidi Peppermint: "Real Toads" appeared in *La Petite Zine*. Reprinted by permission of the poet.

Bob Perelman: "Here 2" appeared in *DCPoetry Anthology 2003*. Reprinted by permission of the poet.

Carl Phillips: "Pleasure" appeared in *Tin House*. Reprinted by permission of the poet.

Robert Pinsky: "Samba" appeared in the *Threepenny Review*. Reprinted by permission of the poet.

Carl Rakosi: "In the First Circle of Limbo" appeared in *American Poetry Review*. Reprinted by permission of the poet.

Ed Roberson: "Ideas Gray Suits Bowler Hats Baal" appeared in *Chicago Review*. Reprinted by permission of the poet.

Kit Robinson: "The 3D Matchmove Artist" appeared in *DCPoetry Anthology 2003*. Reprinted by permission of the poet.